PARABLES
VIRTUAL REALITY

AT A GLANCE

Parables: Virtual Reality
© 1988, 1998 Serendipity House
Eleventh Printing 2011

Published by Serendipity House Publishers
Nashville, Tennessee

ISBN 978-1-5749-4106-7
Item 001201260

Dewey Decimal Classification: 226.8
Subject Headings: BIBLE—PARABLES \ JESUS CHRIST—PARABLES \
BIBLE. N.T.—STUDY AND TEACHING

To purchase additional copies of this resource or other studies:
ORDER ONLINE at *www.SerendipityHouse.com*
WRITE Serendipity House, One LifeWay Plaza, Nashville, TN 37234
FAX (615) 251-5933
PHONE (800) 458-2772

1-800-458-2772
www.SerendipityHouse.com

Printed in the United States of America

WELCOME TO THE SERENDIPITY 301 DEPTH BIBLE STUDY SERIES

You are about to embark on an adventure into the powerful experience of depth Bible Study. The Serendipity 301 series combines three basic elements to produce a life-changing and group-changing course.

First, you will be challenged and enriched by the personal Bible Study that begins each unit. You will have the opportunity to dig into Scripture both for understanding and personal reflection. Although some groups may choose to do this section together at their meeting, doing it beforehand will greatly add to the experience of the course.

Second, you will benefit from the group sessions. Wonderful things happen when a small group of people get together and share their lives around the Word of God. Not only will you have a chance to take your personal study to a deeper level, you will have an opportunity to share on a deep level what's happening in your life and receive the encouragement and prayer support of your group.

Third, the 301 courses provide the stimulus and tools for your group to take steps toward fulfilling your group mission. Whether or not your group has gone through the preparation of a Serendipity 101 and 201 course, you can profit from this mission emphasis. The 32-page center section of this book will guide you through this process. And questions in the closing section of the group agenda will prompt your group to act upon the mission challenge to "give birth" to a new small group.

Put these three components together, and you have a journey in Christian discipleship well worth the effort. Enjoy God's Word! Enjoy genuine Christian community! Enjoy dreaming about your mission!

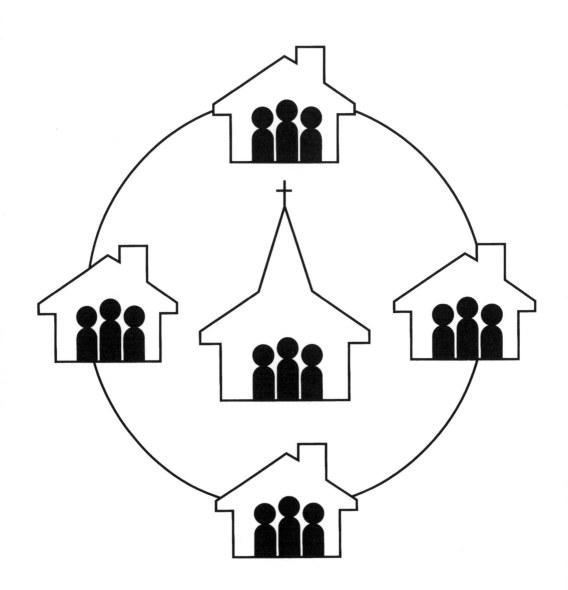

QUESTIONS & ANSWERS

STAGE

1. What stage in the life cycle of a small group is this course designed for?

Turn to the first page of the center section of this book. There you will see that this 301 course is designed for the third stage of a small group. In the Serendipity "Game Plan" for the multiplication of small groups, your group is in the Develop Stage.

GOALS

2. What are the goals of a 301 study course?

As shown on the second page of the center section (page M2), the focus in this third stage is heavy on sharing, Bible Study and Mission.

BIBLE STUDY

301

3. What is the approach to Bible Study in this course?

This course involves two types of Bible Study. The "homework" assignment fosters growth in personal Bible study skills and in personal spiritual growth. The group study gives everyone a chance to share their learning and together take it to a deeper level.

SELF STUDY

4. What does the homework involve?

There are three parts to each assignment: (1) READ—to get the "bird's-eye view" of the passage and record your first impressions; (2) SEARCH—to get the "worm's-eye view" by digging into the passage verse-by-verse with specific questions; and (3) APPLY—to ask yourself, after studying the passage, "What am I going to do about it?"

**FOUR-STAGE
LIFE CYCLE
OF A GROUP**

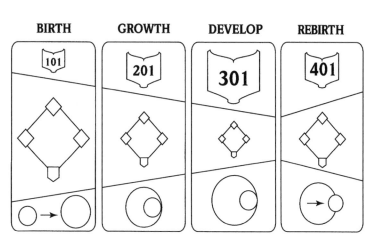

| BIRTH | GROWTH | DEVELOP | REBIRTH |

BIBLE KNOWLEDGE

5. *What if you don't know very much about the Bible?*

No problem. The homework assignment is designed to lead you step-by-step in your study. And there are study notes in each unit to give you help with key words, concepts and difficult passages.

AGENDA

6. *What is the agenda for the group meetings?*

The completed homework assignment becomes the basis for the group sharing. (However, those who don't do the homework should definitely be encouraged to come to the meeting anyway.) During the meeting the group will be guided to share on three levels: (1) TO BEGIN; (2) TO GO DEEPER; and (3) TO CLOSE.

STAYING ON TRACK

7. *How can the group get through all the material?*

Following the recommended time limits for each of the three sections will help keep you on track. Since you may not be able to answer all the questions with the time you have, you may need to skip some of them. Also, if you have more than nine people at a meeting, use the "Subgrouping" described below for the Bible Study.

SUBGROUPING

If you have nine or more people at a meeting, Serendipity recommends you divide into groups of 4–6 for the Bible Study. Count off around the group: "one, two, one, two, etc."—and have the "ones" move quickly to another room for the Bible Study. Ask one person to be the leader and follow the directions for the Bible Study time. After 30 minutes, the Group Leader will call "Time" and ask all subgroups to come together for the Caring Time.

GROUP BUILDING

8. *How does this course develop Group Building?*

Although this series is one of Serendipity's deepest Bible Study curriculum, Group Building is still essential. The group will continue "checking in" with each other and will challenge each other to grow in Christian discipleship. Working together on the group's mission should also be a very positive group-building process.

MISSION / MULTIPLICATION

9. *What is the mission of a 301 group?*

Page M3 of the center section summarizes the mission of groups using this course: to get ready to commission a team (happens in the fourth stage: Rebirth) from your group to start a new group. The center section will lead your group in doing this.

10. *How do we incorporate this mission into the course?*

Page M5 of the center section gives an overview of the six steps in this process. You can either add this leadership training to the sessions a little bit at a time or in a couple of separate sessions.

11. *What is a group covenant?*

A group covenant is a "contract" that spells out your expectations and the ground rules for your group. It's very important that your group discuss these issues—preferably as part of the first session (also see page M32 in the center section).

12. *What are the ground rules for the group?* (Check those that you agree upon.)

❏ PRIORITY: While you are in this course of study, you give the group meetings priority.

❏ PARTICIPATION: Everyone is encouraged to participate and no one dominates.

❏ RESPECT: Everyone is given the right to his or her own opinion, and all questions are encouraged and respected.

❏ CONFIDENTIALITY: Anything that is said in the meeting is never repeated outside the meeting.

❏ LIFE CHANGE: We will regularly assess our own life change goals and encourage one another in our pursuit of Christlikeness.

❏ EMPTY CHAIR: The group stays open to reaching new people at every meeting.

❏ CARE & SUPPORT: Permission is given to call upon each other at any time especially in times of crisis. The group will provide care for every member.

❏ ACCOUNTABILITY: We agree to let the members of the group hold us accountable to the commitments which each of us make in whatever loving ways we decide upon.

❏ MISSION: We will do everything in our power to start a new group.

❏ MINISTRY: The group will encourage one another to volunteer and serve in a ministry, and to support missions by giving financially and/or personally serving.

INTRODUCTION TO THE PARABLES

"He taught them many things by parables ..." (Mark 4:2).

Jesus was a master storyteller. Whether he was addressing a large crowd on a hillside, sharing a private meal with his disciples, or answering one of the Pharisees' trick questions, Jesus would often use stories to make his point.

Jesus used other methods of teaching, of course. He gave lectures and sermons, he posed thought-provoking questions, and he debated and dialogued. But there was something unique about the stories he told. Though simple in form, these stories carried a deeper message that slowly penetrated the minds of his listeners until the truth of it exploded within them. Some people were enlightened and compelled to glorify God. Others were enraged when they realized what Jesus was really saying about them and about himself.

These stories—or parables—have a lasting quality about them. They not only challenged the original hearers to consider seriously their relationship with God, they also cause us to do the same. In this book, we will be studying 13 of Jesus' best-known parables. But before we begin, we need to consider a few details about parables in general—their meaning, purpose and interpretation.

What Is a Parable?

The English word "parable" comes from the Greek word *parabole*, which literally means "to place alongside." So, a parable compares one thing to another. In the Gospels, they are specifically used to compare some aspect of common, everyday life with some reality about the kingdom of God. However, parables are not simply illustrations (such as those found in modern speech or sermons). An illustration may help an audience understand or apply a point the speaker is making, but it is not in itself essential to what the speaker is trying to say; the main weight of the communication is carried by concepts and ideas. In contrast, a parable is the message. It is not used to illustrate the point; it is the point. In graphic, picturesque language the parable communicates insight about God, his kingdom, and the response expected of those who hear.

There is no single, uniform type of parable. In the Greek version of the Old Testament, the word parable is applied to proverbs (1 Sam. 10:12; Prov. 1:1,6), riddles (Judges 14:10–18), taunt songs (Micah 2:4; Hab. 2:6ff) and allegories (Isa. 5:1–7; Ezek. 17:3–24).[1] The same broad use of the word is found in the New Testament, where parables range from short one-liners (e.g., "It is not the healthy who need a doctor, but the sick"—Mark 2:17) to extended narratives like the story of the Good Samaritan (Luke 10:25–37). Parables are not unique to Jesus. Parables such as those Jesus told can be found in the Old Testament, and in the literature of Jewish rabbis (prior to Jesus) who used parables as a means of teaching. While the breadth of the nature and purpose of parables makes definition difficult, there are two helpful definitions:

- A metaphor or simile drawn from life or nature which captures our interest (by being so vivid and strange) and leaves us just enough confused (and teased) to think deeply about what it exactly means for our lives.[2]

- A dramatic form of theological language that compels us to make a response, because it reveals the nature of the kingdom of God (or shows how a child of the kingdom should act).[3]

The Purpose of the Parables

Both definitions emphasize how the parables of Jesus call for response. Parables are not simply stories (like Aesop's fables) that reinforce the kind of moral values that contribute to a good life. Nor are they Zen riddles meant to unhinge our minds to prepare us to transcend levels of consciousness. Instead, as the second definition shows, their intent is to reveal something of the kingdom of God and to call the hearer to respond to Jesus and his mission. They describe what life in that kingdom is like. They portray something of the nature of the King. They call the listeners to decide how they will live in light of the presence of the King in their midst. As has been often observed, no one would have bothered to crucify an itinerant Jewish peasant who went around telling stories that encouraged proper moral behavior! No—the parables are stories of a new kingdom that stands against the old ways.

While it is popularly thought that Jesus used parables to simplify hard truths, the reality is that the parables themselves were difficult to understand! As noted in the first definition, one mark of many of Jesus' parables is that they have a twist that would have been totally unexpected to his hearers, and disturbed their assumptions about the way things are. A Samaritan, despised by the orthodox Jews as unworthy of God, ends up as the hero in a story that includes Jewish priests and Levites. Despotic, fabulously wealthy kings, normally concerned only with their own power and wealth, mercifully cancel enormous debts owed to them by mere servants who have wasted the king's resources. People throw a party over the recovery of one stupid lamb that got lost from a herd. As Jesus speaks to the Middle Eastern listener of his day, he knows that none of these actions are normal. It is precisely these strange twists that make the parables like thought-bombs which are tossed into the lives of those who hear them. Some parables may have a short fuse and others may have a long one, but sooner or later the parable explodes, rocking the hearer with new awareness about the implications of Jesus and his kingdom. In these parables "the ordinary has gone askew and thereby shocks us into realizing that the parables lead into another way of thinking about life."[4]

Craig Blomberg provides a helpful summary of the overall purposes of the parables:

1. Jesus has three main topics of interest: the graciousness of God, the demands of discipleship, and the dangers of disobedience.

2. The central theme uniting all of the lessons of the parables is the kingdom of God. It is both present and future ... It involves both personal transformation and social reform. It is ... the dynamic power of God's personal revelation of himself in creating a human community of those who serve Jesus in every area of their lives.

3. The teachings of the parables raise the question of Jesus' identity. Who is this one who, by his teaching, can claim to forgive sins, pronounce God's blessing on social outcasts, and declare that final judgment will be based on the responses people make to him?

4. Jesus' parables include implicit claims to deity. Jesus associates himself with authority figures in his parables (which obviously stand for the God of the Hebrew Scriptures). His audiences must decide whether to accept these claims and worship him, or to reject them as misguided or even blasphemous. But Jesus' parables leave no neutral ground for casual interest or idle curiosity. They sharply divided their original audiences into disciples and opponents. They must continue to function in the same way today.[5]

Interpreting the Parables

For much of the history of the church, the parables were seen as elaborate allegories. In an allegory, the details of a story have a deeper meaning that the reader must discern. While a few of the parables in the Gospels are interpreted allegorically by Jesus himself (i.e., Matt. 13:24–30,36–43), this approach to the parables led some interpreters to assign meanings to details that had no relation to anything that Jesus' original hearers would have understood. The danger in treating parables as allegories is that the parables can then be manipulated to support whatever theological interests are important to the reader, rather than allowing them to convey the original intention of Jesus.

The allegorical approach was finally challenged by leaders of the Reformation period. Calvin, Luther and others sought to understand parables within the context of Jesus' ministry. But even they often failed to understand much of what Jesus was saying. It wasn't until the 19th century that scholars began to study these teachings in light of the historical, cultural and theological realities of Jesus' time. Since then, in reaction to the excessive, fanciful allegorizing of the parables that dominated earlier periods of the church, the prevailing position has been that parables have only one main point, and that this point is somehow related to the kingdom of God.

While this was a needed corrective, today there are scholars who argue that this perspective is too limited. These scholars have opened the way to looking for multiple meanings in the parables, not in the sense that they become imaginative allegories, but in the sense that the various characters and situations in the parables are meant to embrace various theological themes that work together to evoke a response from the hearer.

Kenneth Bailey suggests several important principles to keep in mind in seeking to understand, interpret and apply a parable:

1. *Determine the audience.* Is Jesus talking to the scribes and Pharisees, to the crowds, or to his disciples? The meaning of the parable is related to the audience who heard it. The Parable of the Prodigal Son (Luke 15:11–32) takes on new meaning when it is realized that Jesus told it to a group of Pharisees who were appalled by his association with people they considered to be sinners. Knowing this, the fact that we are not told how the older brother in the story finally responds takes on a new significance. What on one level is the story of God's grace to sinners is, on another level, an open-ended challenge for these Pharisees (who are like the older brother) to repent.

2. *Examine carefully the setting / interpretation provided by the author or his source.* Most of the parables are found in the context of a particular setting which informs the meaning of the parable. For example, the parable about the generous moneylender (Luke 7:41–42) takes on special meaning when we see that it is found in the context of Jesus' encounter with a sinful woman and a self-righteous Pharisee. The context makes it clear that this simple story is a strong rebuke of the lack of love for God on the part of the Pharisee. It also forces the reader to ask questions regarding the authority and identity of Jesus, since he clearly places himself in the role of the one who forgives enormous debts owed to him.

3. *Try to discern the cultural presuppositions of the story, keeping in mind that the people in them are Palestinian peasants.* The point here is not only to identify Middle Eastern customs (such as what people wore or how they traveled), but also to become familiar with *their* values, *their* ways of relating to one another, and *their* sense of propriety. While we in our culture do not see anything particularly strange with older men running (they are either exercising or are about to miss their plane!), older men in the Middle East always walked slowly as a sign of their dignity. This sheds new light on the detail in the Parable of the Prodigal Son which tells how the father *ran* to greet his son.

4. *Try to discern what symbols the original audience would have instinctively identified in the parable.* This process requires us to get into someone else's world. To speak of Santa Claus in the United States is to evoke a whole range of images and feelings that are culturally associated with Santa Claus. However, a man from China would not react the same way to such a comment, since Santa plays no part in Chinese culture. We do not immediately grasp the meanings of the symbols in the same way as the original listeners would have, because we do not share their culture. We have to work at it.

5. *Determine what response the original audience is pressed to make in the original telling of the parable.* As we see the effect the parable was intended to have upon its audience, we can consider what parallel effects it is to have upon us. St. Augustine's interpretation of the Parable of the Good Samaritan laid stress on the importance of getting people into the church in order to be saved. However, since the scribe who asked the question that prompted the parable (Luke 10:25–29) would have understood Jesus' story as a call for him to start acting as a neighbor to anyone in need, it is clear that Augustine's application is invalid. As important as the church is, involvement in it simply is not the topic of this parable.

6. *Discern what the parable says about the cluster of theological themes that it affirms and/or presupposes.* The parables reflect truths about God and how God expects his followers to live. Once we have identified the major symbols the original listeners would have understood and have discerned the response that the parable calls forth on the part of its listeners, we can discern the central truths about God and discipleship which are encapsulated within the parable. For example, Bailey suggests that the parable about the obedient servant in Luke

17:7–10 is built upon the assumptions that the believer is expected to obey God as his servant, that salvation is a gift not a reward, that believers have no claim upon God, and that God is served as one obeys Jesus.

Some of these suggestions may make us feel that there is no way we can understand the parables. After all, most of us have no idea what cultural assumptions or values a Middle Eastern peasant at the time of Jesus might have had! Fortunately, this gap can be filled in through three main ways.

First, we can engage in thoughtful, careful reading of the text to see what it says and what it stresses. Discovering the context of a parable and the responses it generated among people is not difficult, since most of the parables occur in the middle of a bigger story. We can read around the parable to see how it fits into the bigger picture of what is happening. The more we read the Bible, the more familiar we will become with the way people thought and felt at the time. This will help us keep the parables in their historical context and protect us from reading our own thoughts and ideas into them. (The questions for personal study in this book will help you ask the right kinds of questions for this type of careful reading.)

Secondly, we can avail ourselves of the many excellent tools available to help us understand the background of the Bible and its ancient Middle Eastern culture. Bible dictionaries, commentaries, studies of the culture of biblical times (such as the *Life and Times of Jesus* by Alfred Eidersheim), and books on the parables are invaluable aids in this process. The notes that accompany each study are drawn from such resources and the bibliography in this book provides a good reading list for more comprehensive study.

Thirdly, we can benefit from learning about Middle Eastern people and cultures of today. Kenneth Bailey points out that many of the peasant customs and attitudes in the Middle East today have remained relatively unchanged for centuries. The insights about relationships and values that we can learn from Middle Eastern people today can shed valuable light on the meaning of the parables.[6]

Conclusion

The parables remain a rich source of spiritual insight for us. While most North Americans are more used to hearing their theology expressed in creeds and concepts (such as "I believe in God the Father Almighty, maker of heaven and earth ..." or "The chief purpose of man is to glorify God and enjoy him forever"), the parables present us with pictures of God and his kingdom. Like any good art, the parables communicate beyond their original audience. While rooted in the life and times of Jesus, the realities about God and discipleship that the parables present transcend that culture, and speak to us as well in images that are more powerful than words. We may well forget the formal definition of God (found in the catechisms that we were forced to memorize in church school), but we are not likely to forget the parable which tells us that God is like a shepherd who goes to great lengths to find his lost sheep. Those long sermons about what it really means to be a Christian may fade from our memory, but we will remember that the people of the kingdom are like the man who found a treasure buried in a field and in his joy sold all that he had in order to buy the field and gain the treasure. Theological discussions about the end times may leave us suspecting that everyone is really using Bible texts to suit their own perspectives, but we can find a clear word of hope in the assurance that the kingdom of God is like a little bit of yeast in a batch of dough which ends up influencing every part of that dough.

The parables are word pictures Jesus painted in order to teach us theology in a way that would stick with us. Once the parable is heard, it is etched in the mind, where the Spirit of God can, over time, reveal its deeper implications to us as we are prepared to hear them. "He who has ears to hear, let him hear" (Mark 4:9).

[1] John Donahue, *The Gospel in Parable* (Philadelphia, PA: Fortress Press, 1988), p. 5.
[2] Adapted from C.H. Dodd, quoted in *The Gospel in Parable* (ibid., p. 5).
[3] Adapted from Bailey, *Poet and Peasant: Through Peasant Eyes* (Grand Rapids, MI: Eerdmans, 1983).
[4] Donahue, op cit.
[5] Craig Blomberg, *Interpreting the Parables* (InterVarsity Press), pp. 326–327.
[6] Adapted from Bailey, *Poet and Peasant: Through Peasant Eyes*, pp. xxii-xxiiii.

UNIT 1—The Pharisee & Tax Collector / Luke 18:9-14

The Parable of the Pharisee and the Tax Collector

⁹To some who were confident of their own righteousness and looked down on everybody else, Jesus told this parable: ¹⁰"Two men went up to the temple to pray, one a Pharisee and the other a tax collector. ¹¹The Pharisee stood up and prayed about ͣ himself: 'God, I thank you that I am not like other men—robbers, evildoers, adulterers—or even like this tax collector. ¹²I fast twice a week and give a tenth of all I get.'

¹³"But the tax collector stood at a distance. He would not even look up to heaven, but beat his breast and said, 'God, have mercy on me, a sinner.'

¹⁴"I tell you that this man, rather than the other, went home justified before God. For everyone who exalts himself will be humbled, and he who humbles himself will be exalted."

ͣ11 Or *to*

READ

Two readings of the passage are suggested—each with a response to be checked or filled in on the worksheet.

First Reading / First Impressions: To get familiar with the passage as though you are reading this passage for the first time and to record your "first impressions" on the worksheet. What is your immediate reaction to:

> **The Pharisee:**
>
> **The Tax Collector:**

Second Reading / Big Idea: To get the overall idea, thought or "gist" of the passage, as though you are seeing the action from the press box—high above the stadium. What strikes you as the message of this parable?

- ❏ God hates self-righteous religion.
- ❏ God loves humble repentance.
- ❏ Good works can't earn salvation.
- ❏ God knows what's in our hearts.

SEARCH

1. Jesus makes a stark contrast in this parable between two kinds of people. Who was the culturally respectable person, and why was the other person so disrespected (see notes on vv. 9–10)?

2. What attitudes, beliefs or values made the Pharisee feel so superior?

3. How did the tax collector feel about his standing before God?

4. Why is the tax collector the one who goes away justified, or in right standing, before God (see note on v. 14)?

5. How can a person humble himself / herself before God?

APPLY

1. As you begin this course, what are some goals you would like to work on? Check one or two from the list below and add another if you wish.
   - ❒ to get to know God in a more personal way
   - ❒ to understand what I believe as a Christian and where I stand on issues
   - ❒ to develop my skills in Bible study and personal devotions
   - ❒ to belong to a small group that will support me in my growth
   - ❒ to think through my values and priorities in light of God's will
   - ❒ to wrestle with the next step in my spiritual journey

2. What are you willing to commit to in the way of disciplines during the time you are in this course?
   - ❒ to complete the Bible Study home assignment before the group meets
   - ❒ to attend the group meetings except in cases of emergency
   - ❒ to share in leading the group—taking my turn in rotation
   - ❒ to keep confidential anything that is shared in the group
   - ❒ to reach out to others who are not in a group and invite them to join us
   - ❒ to participate in the group's mission of "giving birth" to a new group (see center section)

GROUP AGENDA

Every group meeting has three parts: (1) To Begin (10–15 minutes) to break the ice; (2) To Go Deeper (30 minutes) for Bible Study; and (3) To Close (15–30 minutes) for caring and prayer. When you get to the second part, have someone read the Scripture out loud and then divide into groups of 4 (4 at the dining table, 4 at the kitchen table, etc.). Then have everyone come back together for the third part.

TO BEGIN / 10–15 Min. (Choose 1 or 2)

1. What motivated you to join this group?

2. In high school, what did it take to be part of the "in crowd"? How close did you get?

3. Where is your favorite place to pray?

TO GO DEEPER / 30 Min. (Choose 2 or 3)

1. How do each of the men in this parable see themselves? How sincere do you think each of them were?

2. What question from the homework assignment stands out to you?

3. If you are really honest, in what religious practices or accomplishments do you take pride?

4. When was the first time you cried out, "God, have mercy on me, a sinner"? When was the last time?

5. Right now, considering your attitudes toward others and your reason for being accepted by God, are you more like the Pharisee or the tax collector?

6. CASE STUDY: Dan is a pastor. He also has a problem with pornography, which he keeps secret. To overcome his addiction, he works harder and harder and preaches tougher and tougher about keeping your mind "pure." What *should* Dan do?

TO CLOSE / 15–30 Min.

1. What did you check under APPLY for the goals you would like to work on during this course? What disciplines are you willing to commit to (second question in APPLY)?

2. With whom can you be really open and share your problems? How do you feel about opening up with this group?

3. How would you like the group to pray for you?

NOTES

Summary. This parable relates to the parable that precedes it in Luke 18:1–8 in that it pertains to prayer, but it really belongs more with the two scenes that follow it: Jesus with the little children in verses 15–17 and Jesus and the rich young ruler in verses 18–30. Both the parable and the subsequent scenes revolve around the fact that God's kingdom is given to a far different group of people (little children and the poor) than the ones traditionally thought to have earned it. The parable (vv. 9–14) deals with the attitude of repentant humility required for being right with God, while the two scenes (vv. 15–17; 18–30) emphasize the openness of faith and the absolute commitment to Jesus that is necessary.

18:9 *confident of their own righteousness.* This typifies the attitude of a person who assumes—wrongly—that his or her performance in life satisfies God's standards (Phil. 3:3–9; Gal. 3:10–14).

looked down on everybody else. Literally, this is "to treat with contempt." The Pharisees considered themselves superior to other Jews who were unable (or unwilling) to conform to their detailed interpretation of the Law of Moses.

18:10 *went up to the temple to pray.* Twice daily, the priests at the temple offered a lamb as a sacrifice of atonement for the sins of the people. At these services, people would gather to join in the liturgy and pray.

Pharisee. The Pharisees were a small, powerful religious sect whose prime concern was keeping the Law in all its detail. While modern readers of the NT assume the Pharisees are the "bad guys" in the story, the original audience of this parable respected them as especially devout, godly people.

tax collector. Jesus' listeners would have considered a tax collector as vile as a robber or murderer. Tax collectors were thought to be traitors, because they collaborated with the Roman power in order to become wealthy. Since only the tax collector knew the tax rate required by Rome, he was free to charge whatever the market would bear. Once he paid what he owed Rome, the rest was his to keep.

18:11 *stood up.* This was the typical posture for prayer. The contrast with the position of the tax collector (v. 13) indicates the Pharisee may have stood as closely as possible to the Most Holy Place in the temple, because he assumed the right to draw near to the presence of God.

God, I thank you. To us it is unimaginable that such a prayer might be said in public, yet it would not be unusual for holy men of the time to pray publicly like this. One well-known rabbinic prayer that dates to a time not too long after the time of Jesus reads: "Praised be the Lord that He did not make me a heathen, for all heathen are as nothing before him; praised be He that He did not make me a woman, for woman is not under obligation to fulfill the law; praised be He that He did not make me ... an uneducated man, for the uneducated man is not cautious to avoid sins" (Stott). The Pharisee may have felt it his duty to offer such a prayer aloud as a way of instructing "sinners" in the crowd about the way of righteousness.

I am not like other men. In the Talmud, one rabbi was reported to have been so confident of his own righteousness that were only a hundred saved from judgment, he and his son would be among that number; if only two, then he felt that it would be he and his son!

this tax collector. While the NIV separates the listing of robbers, evildoers and adulterers from the tax collector, the grammar of the verse also allows the entire list to be meant as a reference to the tax collector. They were considered robbers and cheats. Adultery might have been added to highlight the tax collector's sinfulness, or may have been meant figuratively to describe someone who has forsaken loyalty to God. The Pharisee's prayer may well be an attack on the very fact that such a man would dare be present in the temple.

18:12 *I fast twice a week.* While Jews were only required to fast on the Day of Atonement, Pharisees fasted every Monday and Thursday in an attempt to gain merit with God. Although all Jews were expected to give a tithe of one's produce, Pharisees carefully tithed even things that were not required (see

Luke 11:42). This man's external performance of religious obligations was exemplary.

18:13 *stood at a distance.* The tax collector likewise stands apart from the crowd, because he is too ashamed to join them.

beat his breast. Bailey points out that this is an uncommon action for a Middle Eastern man, done only on occasions of great anguish.

have mercy. Literally, this is "make an atonement." In light of the ceremony under way at the temple, the tax collector pleads that the atoning sacrifice might apply to him. He realizes this is his only hope before God.

18:14 *I tell you that this man ... went home justified.* Here is where the listeners would have been surprised. How could it be that the Pharisee, the model of righteousness, is not right before God, whereas the tax collector is forgiven, acquitted by God? The surprising twist in the parable is that righteousness is a matter of humble self-recognition of sin and dependence upon the atonement God provides as a gift (rather than a matter of impressing God with one's performance).

For everyone who exalts himself will be humbled, and he who humbles himself will be exalted. This was a common wisdom saying that echoes a central theme in Jewish teaching about the spiritual life (see 1 Sam. 2:8; Ps. 18:27; Prov. 3:34; Isa. 57:15; Matt. 23:12; Luke 1:52; 14:11). The parable simply reminds the listeners of a truth they should have realized long ago.

UNIT 2—Parable of the Prodigal Son / Luke 15:11-32

The Parable of the Lost Son

¹¹*Jesus continued: "There was a man who had two sons. ¹²The younger one said to his father, 'Father, give me my share of the estate.' So he divided his property between them.*

¹³*"Not long after that, the younger son got together all he had, set off for a distant country and there squandered his wealth in wild living. ¹⁴After he had spent everything, there was a severe famine in that whole country, and he began to be in need. ¹⁵So he went and hired himself out to a citizen of that country, who sent him to his fields to feed pigs. ¹⁶He longed to fill his stomach with the pods that the pigs were eating, but no one gave him anything.*

¹⁷*"When he came to his senses, he said, 'How many of my father's hired men have food to spare, and here I am starving to death! ¹⁸I will set out and go back to my father and say to him: Father, I have sinned against heaven and against you. ¹⁹I am no longer worthy to be called your son; make me like one of your hired men.' ²⁰So he got up and went to his father.*

"But while he was still a long way off, his father saw him and was filled with compassion for him; he ran to his son, threw his arms around him and kissed him.

²¹*"The son said to him, 'Father, I have sinned against heaven and against you. I am no longer worthy to be called your son.'*

²²*"But the father said to his servants, 'Quick! Bring the best robe and put it on him. Put a ring on his finger and sandals on his feet. ²³Bring the fattened calf and kill it. Let's have a feast and celebrate. ²⁴For this son of mine was dead and is alive again; he was lost and is found.' So they began to celebrate.*

²⁵*"Meanwhile, the older son was in the field. When he came near the house, he heard music and dancing. ²⁶So he called one of the servants and asked him what was going on. ²⁷'Your brother has come,' he replied, 'and your father has killed the fattened calf because he has him back safe and sound.'*

²⁸*"The older brother became angry and refused to go in. So his father went out and pleaded with him. ²⁹But he answered his father, 'Look! All these years I've been slaving for you and never disobeyed your orders. Yet you never gave me even a young goat so I could celebrate with my friends. ³⁰But when this son of yours who has squandered your property with prostitutes comes home, you kill the fattened calf for him!'*

³¹*" 'My son,' the father said, 'you are always with me, and everything I have is yours. ³²But we had to celebrate and be glad, because this brother of yours was dead and is alive again; he was lost and is found.' "*

READ

First Reading / First Impressions: Which of these two brothers would you prefer to have as your son? Why?

Second Reading / Big Idea: If you were a reporter covering the younger son's return, what headline would you give this story?
- ❏ "Worthless Bum Comes Home"
- ❏ "Doormat Dad Indulges Delinquent"
- ❏ "Loving Father Amazes All"
- ❏ "Dad Throws Party; Son Throws Fit"
- ❏ other:_____

SEARCH

1. Jesus told this parable, along with two others, to a group of Pharisees who were criticizing his association with tax collectors and sinners. Who do the characters in this parable represent?

The father:	The younger son:	The older brother:

2. Trace the emotional pilgrimage the younger son experienced from his leaving to his return. Other than the first and last stage, which have been filled in for you, how do you think he was feeling?

He leaves▶	Parties▶	Out of money ▶	In the pigpen ▶	Realizes ▶	Returns ▶	He is forgiven
Excited						Accepted
Independent						Thankful
Prideful						Humble
Rebellious						

3. Trace what you think the emotional pilgrimage was for the older son in this parable. What did he feel at each point in this story?

Brother leaves ▶	He stays and works▶	Father longs for brother ▶	Brother's party ▶	Father's plea

4. What point was Jesus making to the Pharisees about the kingdom of God?

5. What does this parable tell us about the nature of God?

APPLY

1. How do you feel about the way God seems to lavishly accept and forgive those who don't seem to deserve it?

2. If you compared your spiritual journey to that of the younger son, where are you now?
   - ❏ never left home
   - ❏ still at home, but itching to check out the "distant country"
   - ❏ in the distant country, trying to have a good time
   - ❏ starting to realize I'm in a pigpen
   - ❏ feeling very alone and far from home
   - ❏ nervously heading home to God, not knowing what to expect
   - ❏ just beginning to feel God's forgiveness
   - ❏ gradually feeling God's acceptance
   - ❏ celebrating with the family of God
   - ❏ other:_____

GROUP AGENDA

Every group meeting has three parts: (1) To Begin (10–15 minutes) to break the ice; (2) To Go Deeper (30 minutes) for Bible Study; and (3) To Close (15–30 minutes) for caring and prayer. When you get to the second part, have someone read the Scripture out loud and then divide into groups of 4 (4 at the dining table, 4 at the kitchen table, etc.). Then have everyone come back together for the third part.

TO BEGIN / 10–15 Min. (Choose 1 or 2)

1. Did you ever run away from home? What happened?

2. Where are you in the birth order of your family?

3. Do you have some of the traits often attributed to the oldest, youngest, middle or only child?

TO GO DEEPER / 30 Min. (Choose 2 or 3)

1. What would you have done if you had been the father in this story when the youngest son asked for his inheritance?

2. If you had been the father and had a pretty good idea where your son had gone, would you have gone after him?

3. Go over as many of the questions in READ and SEARCH as you have time for.

4. What is the closest you have come to going through an experience like this story—either in your relationship with your family or with God?

5. CASE STUDY: Stan has a problem with the baby boomers who are returning to church. They want special groups to help them work through their "prodigal" problems like addictions, compulsions, codependency and being "an adult child of a dysfunctional family." Stan never did leave his faith and doesn't see any reason to deal with these problems. What do you think?

TO CLOSE / 15–30 Min.

1. Who could you invite to this group next week?

2. How did you answer the questions in APPLY?

3. How do you sense God calling you to get closer to him? What will you do to respond?

4. How can the group support you in prayer?

NOTES

Summary. This is the third of three parables in Luke 15 about things that are lost and then found. Marshall notes that this parable "is ... open to a variety of interpretations, dependent on where the main emphasis is thought to lie." For instance, as the Parable of the Loving Father it illustrates the boundless, lavish love of God toward his wayward children (for Old Testament roots of this truth, see Jer. 3:18–20; 31:18–20). As the Parable of the Lost Son it shows the process of repentance and the joy that awaits the sinner who will turn to God. As the Parable of the Older Son it forces the Pharisees to consider the meaning of their own hostility over Jesus' reception of the tax collectors and sinners (Luke 15:1–2).

15:12 *give me my share of the estate.* Under Jewish law, the younger of two sons would receive one-third of the estate upon his father's death (Deut. 21:17). While a father might divide up his property before he died if he wished, this son's request would be considered unbelievably callous and hard-hearted. In essence, he implies that the fact that his father still lives is getting in the way of his plans. The father was under no obligation whatsoever to grant this request; the audience would expect a father faced with such an insulting request to respond with anger. Instead, this father goes along with the request and divides the property between his sons.

15:13 *got together all he had.* In other words, the younger son sold off his share of the estate so that he could have cold, hard cash to do with what he wanted! Such an action would have been scandalous at a time when a person's identity and future was tied up with his family's land. For the sake of satisfying immediate pleasures, he has separated himself from his family, thrown away his means of income, and robbed any children he may have in the future of the security of owning land.

15:15 *hired himself out ... to feed pigs.* Jews considered pigs to be ceremonially unclean animals (Lev. 11:7) and would not eat, raise or touch them. There was even the pronouncement of a curse upon the person who cared for them (Hendriksen).

15:16 *He longed to fill his stomach with the pods that the pigs were eating.* While eating the food of pigs sounds terrible even to modern readers, for the Pharisees in this audience it would have been utterly horrifying. Jesus has painted a picture of an unbelievably arrogant, unpleasant, immoral, foolish, and irreligious young man.

15:19 no longer worthy to be called your son. The son realized that he had no legal, moral or relational claim on his father's goodwill.

hired men. These were day laborers employed only as the day-to-day work of the estate demanded.

15:20 Just as the actions of the son scandalized the Pharisees, so the response of the father violated their understanding of how such a son should be treated.

his father saw him. The implication is that the father had been waiting and hoping to one day see his son return.

was filled with compassion. There is no haughtiness of wounded pride, but only the welling up of pity, love and joy.

ran to his son. Protocol and dignity is thrown to the wind as the father races to his son. Social customs dictated that it was degrading for an elderly man to run to anyone, especially to someone who had so disgraced him. This picture presents an absolutely unique, staggering insight into the response of the Almighty Holy God to a repentant sinner. Bailey comments that in the village setting of this parable, the villagers would have gathered around when they heard the son was returning in order to taunt him for his foolishness. While the son expected to face such taunts, he would have been shocked to see his father welcome him instead, thus sheltering him from the insults of the townspeople.

kissed him. While this was a typical greeting for men, it would have been thought inappropriate given the son's grave offense against his father.

15:21 I am no longer worthy to be called your son. Although the son may have thought he could earn his way back into some relationship with his father in order to alleviate his own misery, at this point he reflects a true sense of repentance: He can offer nothing except a contrite spirit (Ps. 51:17).

15:22 the best robe. This would have been the father's best robe. This is a sign that people should honor him as they honor the father.

a ring. The signet ring gives the son the authority to represent the father.

sandals. Being shoeless was a sign of a slave. To wear shoes indicated a man was free to go where he pleased. Thus the son is immediately and unconditionally elevated to a position of honor and respect in the home.

15:23 fattened calf. This was "an animal specially fed and kept to be slaughtered on a special occasion" (Marshall). The fact that it was a calf that was prepared indicates that the whole village was invited to come to the feast (for such provisions could feed 100 people).

15:24 was dead. It was as if the son were dead (in the sense that he apparently had no intention to live in relationship with his father ever again).

15:25–32 The focus of the parable shifts to the older son (who represents the Pharisees).

15:28 This son was furious at the treatment his younger brother received. He could only see that the father had violated all the customs of how such a wayward son should be treated. His refusal to enter the house would have been seen as a sign of grave disrespect, since the eldest son was expected to play the part of a gracious host at a family feast. As he did with the younger son, the father "went out" to "plead with" the older son. This too was an overwhelming display of grace, since his son's refusal to come to the party was a serious social insult. The parable's listeners would have expected the father to be enraged.

15:29 While the father's love wrought humility in the younger son, the older son responds with even more insulting behavior.

Look! This would have been considered an extremely rude way for a son to address his father, since there is no hint of respect or affection.

I've been slaving for you. Ironically, this son views his ongoing relationship with his father in the way the younger son hoped he might be privileged to have. While always in the vicinity of the father, the older son never enjoyed the relationship with his father that was available to him.

never disobeyed your orders. While there was the appearance of cooperation with the father, this son apparently viewed things in terms of a master/slave relationship. This reflected the Pharisees' reliance upon external conformity to God's Law as the measure by which one could earn God's blessing.

you never gave me. This observation ignores that he has always been in the position to enjoy the love of his father, whereas the younger son has not.

15:31–32 We are not told what the older son did. Jesus left the story open-ended to force the Pharisees to fill in the ending by their behavior.

UNIT 3—The Parable of the Sower / Mark 4:1-20

The Parable of the Sower

4 Again Jesus began to teach by the lake. The crowd that gathered around him was so large that he got into a boat and sat in it out on the lake, while all the people were along the shore at the water's edge. ²He taught them many things by parables, and in his teaching said: ³"Listen! A farmer went out to sow his seed. ⁴As he was scattering the seed, some fell along the path, and the birds came and ate it up. ⁵Some fell on rocky places, where it did not have much soil. It sprang up quickly, because the soil was shallow. ⁶But when the sun came up, the plants were scorched, and they withered because they had no root. ⁷Other seed fell among thorns, which grew up and choked the plants, so that they did not bear grain. ⁸Still other seed fell on good soil. It came up, grew and produced a crop, multiplying thirty, sixty, or even a hundred times."

⁹Then Jesus said, "He who has ears to hear, let him hear."

¹⁰When he was alone, the Twelve and the others around him asked him about the parables. ¹¹He told them, "The secret of the kingdom of God has been given to you. But to those on the outside everything is said in parables ¹²so that,

" 'they may be ever seeing but never perceiving,
  and ever hearing but never understanding;
  otherwise they might turn and be forgiven!'ᵃ "

¹³Then Jesus said to them, "Don't you understand this parable? How then will you understand any parable? ¹⁴The farmer sows the word. ¹⁵Some people are like seed along the path, where the word is sown. As soon as they hear it, Satan comes and takes away the word that was sown in them. ¹⁶Others, like seed sown on rocky places, hear the word and at once receive it with joy. ¹⁷But since they have no root, they last only a short time. When trouble or persecution comes because of the word, they quickly fall away. ¹⁸Still others, like seed sown among thorns, hear the word; ¹⁹but the worries of this life, the deceitfulness of wealth and the desires for other things come in and choke the word, making it unfruitful. ²⁰Others, like seed sown on good soil, hear the word, accept it, and produce a crop—thirty, sixty or even a hundred times what was sown."

ᵃ12 Isaiah 6:9,10

READ

First Reading / First Impressions: What is your first impression of this passage?

❏ This sounds like an article from *Better Homes and Gardens*.

❏ Why does Jesus want to keep some people in the dark?

❏ I'm glad Jesus interprets the parable.

❏ I wonder which soil I am.

Second Reading / Big Idea: In one sentence, what does Jesus seem to be saying is the key to living a "productive" life?

SEARCH

1. List the four types of soils in this parable and the resulting crop produced (see notes on vv. 4–8).

	Soil Type	Resulting Crop
1.		
2.		
3.		
4.		

2. In Jesus' interpretation of the parable (vv. 14–20), he shows the disciples that each soil represents a level of receptivity that people have to his message. Describe the four levels of personal receptivity to the word.

path (v. 15)

rocky (vv. 16–17)

thorns (vv. 18–19)

good (v. 20)

3. Verse 13 indicates that even the disciples did not understand this parable. In verses 9–13, what is Jesus saying about people being open to hear, understand and accept his word (see notes)?

APPLY
Rate yourself by circling an answer on the following scales.

1. When it comes to being open and responsive to Jesus' instruction for my life, I am:

hard as a rock	becoming aware that I need to be open	taking steps to be more open	open and responsive

2. When it comes to growing a root system for my faith, I am:

pretty shallow	becoming aware that I need to grow in my faith	taking steps to grow deeper in my faith	developing deep roots

3. When it comes to the amount of distracting thorns I allow in my life, I am:

getting choked	becoming aware of many thorns	taking steps to remove the thorns	free of thorns

4. When it comes to producing a crop in my life, I am:

without fruit	becoming aware that I have this responsibility	taking steps to bear fruit	yielding a good crop

GROUP AGENDA

Every group meeting has three parts: (1) To Begin (10–15 minutes) to break the ice; (2) To Go Deeper (30 minutes) for Bible Study; and (3) To Close (15–30 minutes) for caring and prayer. When you get to the second part, have someone read the Scripture out loud and then divide into groups of 4 (4 at the dining table, 4 at the kitchen table, etc.). Then have everyone come back together for the third part.

TO BEGIN / 10–15 Min. (Choose 1 or 2)

1. Where were you living when you were 7 years old? What was your yard like?

2. How are you at growing plants?

3. What project have you started but not finished?

TO GO DEEPER / 30 Min. (Choose 2 or 3)

1. Have each person choose one of the questions in READ or SEARCH to answer.

2. Do you think a person is one kind of "soil" throughout his or her life? How about you? What has the "soil" been like at different times in your life?

3. In the period of your life when you produced the best crop, what were the main reasons? When you produced the worst crop, what were the main reasons?

4. Which of the four soils best describes the condition of your heart right now?

5. CASE STUDY: Your pastor is discouraged about the people who have dropped out of the church or who just aren't interested in more than a very minimal commitment. What does this parable have to say about this?

TO CLOSE / 15–30 Min.

1. Has your group started on the six steps toward fulfilling your mission—from the center section?

2. What did you learn about yourself in the APPLY self-inventory?

3. What specific "thorn of worry" would you like the group to pray with you about?

NOTES

Summary. The emphasis in the so-called Parable of the Sower is really on the soils. The parable fits into the context of Mark's Gospel. In chapter 3, Mark records four responses to Jesus: (1) the Pharisees want to kill him (3:6), and accuse him of being demon-possessed (3:22); (2) the crowd seeks him out as a miracle worker to be employed for their purposes (3:7–11); (3) his family, concerned that things are getting out of hand, thinks he is mad (3:21); (4) some people sit at his feet to listen and practice his teaching (3:34–35). The four soils represent the four kinds of responses to Jesus seen thus far in the Gospel. They also foreshadow the kinds of responses that are to come later on. It can also be helpful to consider the parable (vv. 3–8) by itself in order to find what else Jesus might have been implying about the kingdom through the story. For instance, what does it imply about proclaiming the message? What does it indicate about the ultimate result of such proclamation? What does it imply about the effectiveness of the word despite the hardships it might encounter?

4:3 sow his seed. Farmers would throw seed into the soil by a broadcast method.

4:4 the path. There were long, hard pathways between the various plots of land. The soil was so packed down that seed could not penetrate the soil and germinate. The birds came along and ate up this seed which just sat on the surface of the ground.

4:5–6 rocky places. Some of the soil covered a limestone base a few inches beneath the surface. Seed that fell here would germinate, but it would not last (since a proper root system could not develop because of the rock).

4:7 thorns. In other parts of the plot there were the roots of weeds. As the seed grew up, so did the weeds (which stunted the growth of the good seed). Although it lived, such seed would not bear fruit.

4:8 good soil. However, some of the seed fell where it was intended.

thirty, sixty, or even a hundred times. The good soil yielded a spectacular crop. The normal yield for a Palestinian field is seven and a half times what is sown, while 10 times is an especially good harvest. This is where the emphasis in the parable lies: not with the unproductive soil but with the miracle crop.

4:9 let him hear. Jesus urges his hearers to ponder his parable. Part of the power of a parable lies in the fact that people must reflect on it in order to understand it.

4:10 The subject of his parables is not yet clear—even to the disciples! Nor in fact will Jesus' teaching become fully clear to the disciples before his death. It is not easy for them (and others) to question their assumptions about the way God works in order to see who Jesus really is and what the kingdom is actually all about.

4:11–12 At first reading, this may appear to be saying that parables are designed to obscure the truth. In fact, this simply states (with some irony) what is a fact: some respond to Jesus and some do not. The teachers of the Law, for example, see Jesus' miracles and hear his teaching, yet they ascribe his power to Satan (Mark 3:22). They see but do not perceive.

4:11 *The secret ... has been given to you.* A secret in the New Testament is not something which is hidden; rather, it is something which was previously unknown but has now been revealed to all who will hear. The secret given the disciples is that the kingdom of God has come. Not even the disciples perceive fully what is going on (v. 13). To be "given the secret" means something like "called to follow Jesus." It is as the disciples follow Jesus that they will come to understand more fully what he means.

those on the outside. The point is not that God calls some and excludes others. Rather, those who are on the outside are simply those who fail to pursue the kingdom. The secret is open to all who, like the disciples, ask.

4:12 *ever seeing / ever hearing.* This quote is from Isaiah 6:9–10 (in which God called the prophet to speak his word, even though Israel would not listen). Although they saw God's messenger and heard his word, they refused to heed his message.

otherwise they might turn and be forgiven. It was not that God did not want people to repent as a result of the preaching of Isaiah. This verse can only be understood when one sees it as full of irony, a characteristic of Isaiah's writing. From God's perspective, the behavior of the people is such that it seems the last thing they want to do is actually experience God's forgiveness. Jesus uses this quote to indicate the same thing is happening in his day. Those on the outside are those who refuse to see and hear what he is saying because they do not want to change their ways.

4:13–20 This is the only parable interpreted in this Gospel. Mark helps the reader understand the four types of responses to Jesus seen thus far in the Gospel. From 3:7–35, it would appear that two responses to Jesus are negative (the teachers of the Law and the family) and two positive (the crowds and the Twelve). But here in this parable it becomes clear that only one response (that of the Twelve) will bear fruit for the kingdom.

4:14 The seed is the message of God's kingdom.

4:15 Some, like the teachers of the Law, are so hardened (like the soil on the paths between plots) that the seed of the word never penetrates. It is, instead, snatched away by Satan before it can germinate.

Satan. The teachers of the Law have charged Jesus with being dominated by Satan. However, it turns out that they are the ones under his influence!

4:16–17 Others, like the crowds, are superficially attracted to Jesus. They like what he can give them (powerful teaching, healing of disease, casting out of demons), but the level of their commitment is not deep. It will fall away as soon as there is any hint of persecution.

4:16 *receive it with joy.* Indeed, the common people flocked to Jesus once they saw what he could do (see Mark 1:16–45; 3:7–12).

4:18–19 Still others, like his family, allow the wrong concerns (Is he eating properly? What gives him the right to fancy himself a rabbi?) to squeeze out the growing plant (see Mark 3:20–21,31–35; 6:1–6).

4:19 *the deceitfulness of wealth and the desires for other things.* Following Jesus requires wholehearted loyalty to him. Money and the "other things" in view here are not evil in themselves, the disciple is warned not to allow anything else to take priority over hearing and practicing the words of Jesus.

4:20 But in the end, some, like the Twelve, will produce abundant fruit (see Mark 3:13–19).

a crop. The crop in view here is a life full of the qualities of discipleship, such as righteousness, love, joy, peace, goodness, etc. (Gal. 5:22–23; Phil. 1:11).

thirty, sixty or even a hundred times. While it may appear that there are three types of unproductive soil (hard, rocky, weed-filled) and three types of productive soil (that bearing thirty-fold, sixty-fold and a hundred-fold), in essence the point is that there are only two kinds of soil: unproductive and productive.

UNIT 4—The Unmerciful Servant / Matt. 18:21-35

The Parable of the Unmerciful Servant

²¹*Then Peter came to Jesus and asked, "Lord, how many times shall I forgive my brother when he sins against me? Up to seven times?"*

²²*Jesus answered, "I tell you, not seven times, but seventy-seven times.*ᵃ

²³*"Therefore, the kingdom of heaven is like a king who wanted to settle accounts with his servants.* ²⁴*As he began the settlement, a man who owed him ten thousand talents*ᵇ *was brought to him.* ²⁵*Since he was not able to pay, the master ordered that he and his wife and his children and all that he had be sold to repay the debt.*

²⁶*"The servant fell on his knees before him. 'Be patient with me,' he begged, 'and I will pay back everything.'* ²⁷*The servant's master took pity on him, canceled the debt and let him go.*

²⁸*"But when that servant went out, he found one of his fellow servants who owed him a hundred denarii.*ᶜ *He grabbed him and began to choke him. 'Pay back what you owe me!' he demanded.*

²⁹*"His fellow servant fell to his knees and begged him, 'Be patient with me, and I will pay you back.'*

³⁰*"But he refused. Instead, he went off and had the man thrown into prison until he could pay the debt.* ³¹*When the other servants saw what had happened, they were greatly distressed and went and told their master everything that had happened.*

³²*"Then the master called the servant in. 'You wicked servant,' he said, 'I canceled all that debt of yours because you begged me to.* ³³*Shouldn't you have had mercy on your fellow servant just as I had on you?'* ³⁴*In anger his master turned him over to the jailers to be tortured, until he should pay back all he owed.*

³⁵*"This is how my heavenly Father will treat each of you unless you forgive your brother from your heart."*

ᵃ22 Or *seventy times seven*   ᵇ24 That is, millions of dollars
ᶜ28 That is, a few dollars

READ

First Reading / First Impressions: If you were Peter, what would you have thought after Jesus answered your question?

❏ I don't understand.
❏ This is serious stuff.
❏ This is going to be hard to do.

❏ I'm anxious to give this a try.
❏ I'm sorry I asked!
❏ other:_____

Second Reading / Big Idea: What is the principle here for dealing with someone who has wronged you?

❏ "an eye for an eye"
❏ You can't out-forgive God.
❏ God expects you to be a pushover.

❏ People who can't forgive wind up in their own chains.
❏ Only the forgiven can forgive.
❏ other:_____

SEARCH

1. How do you think those listening to Jesus responded when they heard the enormous amount (see note on v. 24) the first servant owed the king? What would they have expected to happen?

2. How is the master's response in verse 27 symbolic of God's action on our behalf through Jesus (see notes)?

3. Legally, the first servant had every right to do what he did to the man who owed him the money. Given that, on what basis was the king so infuriated when he heard what had happened?

4. The way Jesus told the story, the reader is led to join with the "other servants" who perceived a great injustice here. How does he use that recognition of gross unfairness to drive home the point of the story (see notes on v. 33 and v. 35)?

5. In refusing to be merciful to others, what do we deny ourselves (vv. 32–35)?

6. How does the point of the parable relate to Peter's original question (see note on vv. 23–24)?

APPLY

1. The size of the debt I have had to ask God to forgive me for is ... (Circle one.)

Millions	**Thousands**	**Hundreds**	**Tens**

2. When it comes to "forgiving your debtors," are you closer to the master who forgave or the servant who wouldn't forgive? (Put an **"X"** on the scale.)

The Master	**The Servant**

3. Modeled on God's forgiveness of you, is there someone in your life to whom you need to extend heartfelt forgiveness? What would it mean to do so in a way that he or she would really know your forgiveness?

GROUP AGENDA

After the first part, read the Scripture out loud and divide into groups of 4. Then come back together for the third part.

TO BEGIN / 10–15 Min. (Choose 1 or 2)
1. What was one of the worst things your brother or sister did to you when you were growing up?

2. With your family now, are you more likely to "forgive" their debts, or make them pay up?

3. What would you do to celebrate if all of your debts were suddenly canceled?

TO GO DEEPER / 30 Min. (Choose 2 or 3)
1. If you have completed the homework, what stands out to you from the READ and SEARCH questions or the study notes?

2. Based on this parable, is God's forgiveness of us limited or unlimited? Is it conditional or unconditional? How about our forgiveness of others?

3. What have you found helpful in dealing with someone who has hurt you?

4. Suppose someone said to you (on the basis of this passage), "The problem with you Christians is that you let everybody off the hook. You just don't realize that by doing so you are only encouraging irresponsible behavior." How would you respond?

5. CASE STUDY: When you were growing up, you had to share a bedroom with your little brother, where he kept "his side" like a pigpen. He "borrowed" your clothes without asking, left the car a mess when he used it, and never thought of filling the tank with gas. Now, the two of you run the family business, but you have to keep the books, pay the bills, and come in on Saturdays while he coaches a Little League team. Recently, your doctor told you that you have an ulcer, and it is caused by deep-seated anger against your little brother. What do you do?

TO CLOSE / 15–30 Min.
1. Has your group taken the survey for small groups in your church (see page M15 in the center section)? If so, what will you do as a result?

2. What did you discover about yourself in APPLY? (You don't need to share your response to the third question about who you need to forgive, unless you want to.)

3. How can the group pray for you?

NOTES

Summary. Matthew 18:5–20 introduces the topic of sin, forgiveness and reconciliation. Here, this discussion is continued in order to get at the heart of the reason why the disciple of Jesus is to be merciful and forgiving toward others.

18:21 *how many times shall I forgive my brother when he sins against me? Up to seven times?* The rabbis taught that a person ought to be forgiven for a particular offense up to three times. After that, the offended person was under no obligation to grant forgiveness. Realizing that Jesus had a greater sense of the importance of mercy than was typical for rabbis, Peter was willing to double the traditional amount plus add one more time for good measure! Since seven was considered the number of completion and perfection, Peter may have thought that anyone who could forgive someone that many times would be a spiritually perfect person.

18:22 *seventy-seven times.* This could also be understood as seventy times seven. Whichever reading is correct, by taking what Peter thought was a generous offer and multiplying it in this way, Jesus explodes any notion of a limit to forgiveness! It is probable that "seventy-seven" is the correct reading, since it is the same number found in the Greek version of Genesis 4:24 (which refers to a comment made by Lamech, a violent man and descendant from Cain, the first murderer). Jesus took what was a pattern for ever-increasing vengeance and transformed it to one of ever-increasing forgiveness.

18:23–34 To illustrate the need for forgiveness of others, Matthew includes this parable. While it does not relate to the concern of Peter (about the number of times one ought to forgive someone), it does get to the heart of the matter regarding why the lack of forgiveness is inexcusable for a disciple of Jesus.

18:23–27 Act One of the parable introduces the reader to a king and a servant with a tremendous debt.

18:23 *a king.* Given the amount of money involved and the form of punishment, it is clear that the "king" in view here is no ancient Jewish king. Rather, Jesus is tapping the people's imagination of what the fabulously wealthy kings of Egypt or Persia must have been like.

settle accounts. Kings would entrust the day-to-day affairs of their kingdom to the management of servants (who were responsible for pursuing the king's best interest in their responsibilities). Such a servant might have been the manager of several tax stations responsible for collecting revenue for the king. This was an audit to check on how the servants were doing with respect to their management.

18:24 *ten thousand talents.* This is difficult to translate into an exact modern amount. However, the point is that it is an impossibly high amount, as if a person today was found to be millions (or even billions) of dollars in debt. Herod the Great, who ruled over Palestine at the time of Jesus' birth, had an annual tax revenue of only about 900 talents. The crowd listening to Jesus would have gasped at the thought of having to pay someone such a fantastically high amount of money.

18:25 *he and his wife and his children and all that he had be sold.* Jewish kings could not do this, but "The oriental king was all powerful, possessing the right of life and death over his subjects" (Hill). Thus, the king had the right to divide up the man's family to sell them into slavery to recoup at least a fraction of his losses.

18:26 *I will pay back everything.* This was an impossible promise. While it may reflect his sincere desire to save himself and his family, it was beyond his ability to carry out.

18:27 This verse reflects the heart, not only of the king, but of God. The king's actions would have been totally unexpected (given the popular image of cruel, powerful, heartless kings). Instead, here is one who forgave a lowly servant for no reason! The king gained nothing for this action. The twist of the parable at this point is that kings aren't supposed to act like this!

took pity. Elsewhere in Matthew, this same word, translated as "compassion," is used to describe the attitude of Jesus toward the sick (9:36), toward the hungry (15:32), and toward the blind (20:34). Like the man in this story, none of the people Jesus had compassion for were able to do anything about their situation.

canceled the debt. For readers familiar with the meaning of Jesus' death, this allusion to what God has done for sinners through Christ would be inescapable. The NT sometimes pictures sin as a debt owed to God that has been canceled because of God's mercy in Christ (Rom. 6:23; Col. 2:13–15).

18:28–30 This is Act Two. The first servant meets another man who owes him some money. While the reader leaves Act One rejoicing with the servant, Act Two reveals how repulsive he truly is.

18:28 *a hundred denarii.* Since a denarii was a day's wage for a laborer, this is a reasonably large amount. However, it pales into insignificance when compared to the sum the first servant owed the king.

18:29 In words similar to what the first servant had spoken to the king, the second servant promises to repay the debt. In the case of the first servant, such a promise was impossible; in this case repayment could easily have been made over time. The first servant did not need to cancel the debt as had the king; he could have given the second servant some more time.

18:30 *But he refused.* This is the second surprise twist in the parable. Under the circumstances, this man would have been expected to forego the debt. Instead, he insists on carrying out the full weight of the law against the servant indebted to him. The mercy he has received from the king has not produced any new sense of moral character in this man. Instead, he still wants to operate on terms of strict justice.

thrown into prison. In a debtor's prison, the man's assets would have to be sold in order to make payment.

18:31–34 In Act Three, the king is told of the situation and responds in anger. The readers would be in sympathy with the others who told the king about the actions of the first servant. He has violated the mercy of the king by refusing to extend mercy to the second servant. No one would doubt that now his punishment is justly deserved.

18:33 *Shouldn't you have had mercy ... just as I had on you?* This is the point of the parable. As recipients of mercy from God, Christ's disciples are obligated to forgive others continually. Not to do so is as incongruous as is the action of the servant in the story. Not to do so is to reveal that they have not grasped the reality of the mercy they have received from God.

18:34 *to be tortured.* The man will now be pressed for every cent he has.

18:35 The parable is applied to the listeners: As in Matthew 6:14–15, God's forgiveness of us is to shape the way we forgive others. If it does not, we remain under judgment. Thus, Matthew emphasizes the need for the Christian community to be a place where forgiveness is found in abundant supply.

UNIT 5—The Good Samaritan / Luke 10:25-37

The Parable of the Good Samaritan

²⁵On one occasion an expert in the law stood up to test Jesus. "Teacher," he asked, "what must I do to inherit eternal life?"

²⁶"What is written in the Law?" he replied. "How do you read it?"

²⁷He answered: " 'Love the Lord your God with all your heart and with all your soul and with all your strength and with all your mind'ᵃ; and, 'Love your neighbor as yourself.'ᵇ "

²⁸"You have answered correctly," Jesus replied. "Do this and you will live."

²⁹But he wanted to justify himself, so he asked Jesus, "And who is my neighbor?"

³⁰In reply Jesus said: "A man was going down from Jerusalem to Jericho, when he fell into the hands of robbers. They stripped him of his clothes, beat him and went away, leaving him half dead. ³¹A priest happened to be going down the same road, and when he saw the man, he passed by on the other side. ³²So too, a Levite, when he came to the place and saw him, passed by on the other side. ³³But a Samaritan, as he traveled, came where the man was; and when he saw him, he took pity on him. ³⁴He went to him and bandaged his wounds, pouring on oil and wine. Then he put the man on his own donkey, took him to an inn and took care of him. ³⁵The next day he took out two silver coinsᶜ and gave them to the innkeeper. 'Look after him,' he said, 'and when I return, I will reimburse you for any extra expense you may have.'

³⁶"Which of these three do you think was a neighbor to the man who fell into the hands of robbers?"

³⁷The expert in the law replied, "The one who had mercy on him."

Jesus told him, "Go and do likewise."

ᵃ27 Deut. 6:5   ᵇ27 Lev. 19:18   ᶜ35 Greek *two denarii*

READ
First Reading / First Impressions: How would the media respond if something like the story in this parable happened today?

❑ The violence would make big news.

❑ The apathy would make big news.

❑ It would be ignored because stuff like this is so common.

Second Reading / Big Idea: Just from skimming the story, what do you assume is the main point?

SEARCH
1. The "expert in the law" was not asking a sincere question, but was trying to "test Jesus." What do you think is the nature of the test he was giving Jesus?

2. How could the priest and the Levite justify refusing to help this mugging victim (see notes on vv. 30–32)?

3. Rabbinic literature spoke of "priests, Levites, and Israelites" as a way of referring to all social classes among the Jews. The expectation would have been that the third man in the story should be an "Israelite." How would Jesus' Jewish audience have reacted to his casting a despised Samaritan as the hero of the story (see note on v. 33)?

4. What is Jesus' instruction to his followers—who is my neighbor and how am I to love that person?

My neighbor is:

I love by:

5. Who is actually testing who in this passage (see notes on v. 29 and vv. 36–37)?

APPLY

1. Why do most people act like the priest and Levite who passed by the man in need?

2. How often do you find people in your path who need your help? (Circle one.)

quite often	occasionally	seldom	never

3. The Samaritan felt compassion and took action to help. For Jesus, love is something you both feel and do. Place an *"X"* on the scale below where you would see yourself in this regard.

I feel no pity
and take no action.   I feel compassion
                                                             and take action.

GROUP AGENDA

After the first part, read the Scripture out loud and divide into groups of 4. Then come back together for the third part.

TO BEGIN / 10–15 Min. (Choose 1 or 2)

1. What is the worst experience you have had with car trouble? Who came along and helped you?

2. Who was your next-door neighbor when you were growing up? What were they like?

3. Who has been the best neighbor you've ever had? What made them so?

TO GO DEEPER / 30 Min. (Choose 2 or 3)

1. If you have completed READ and SEARCH, choose one of the questions and share your answer. (It's okay if more than one person chooses the same question.)

2. The reasons the priest and the Levite had for bypassing strangers were valid in some cases, but not in this one. Why not? If you were in the same situation, what would you do?

3. If Jesus were to recast this story today, who would the Samaritan be (the last kind of person people would want to see billed as a hero)?

4. What are the biggest problems in your community? If the Good Samaritan came to your community, what would he do about these problems?

5. How willing are you to risk helping someone in need today?

6. CASE STUDY: Joe was released from prison where he "did time" for assault and possession of illegal drugs. He may also have a sexual addiction. Some people in church don't want anything to do with Joe. How could you help Joe? How could you help those who don't want Joe around?

TO CLOSE / 15–30 Min.

1. Are you working on your mission as a group? Are you inviting new people to join you?

2. How did you answer the questions in APPLY, particularly question 3?

3. Who has been a Good Samaritan in your life recently? How can you be a Good Samaritan this week for someone you know who is hurting?

4. How can the group pray for you?

NOTES

Summary. This well-known story is found only in Luke's Gospel. In it Jesus points out how the Jewish leaders, who knew the Law perfectly well, failed to live by it (because of their lack of love for others outside of their own circle).

10:25 *an expert in the law.* The experts in the Torah were charged with the responsibility of interpreting the Law and teaching people what was involved in its observance.

to test Jesus. The respected theologian was checking out just how astute this young, uncertified teacher really was. His question is meant to force Jesus to penetrate into the heart of the multitudinous commandments that made up Jewish tradition: What is the essential command?

What shall I do to inherit eternal life? The rabbis taught that eternal life was gained through the keeping of God's Law, often enumerating various actions that one should follow. The scribe was undoubtedly expecting some such list of requirements that would allow him a basis on which to debate Jesus. Jesus had a reputation among the scribes as one who did not take the Law seriously enough. This would be a chance to trip him up.

10:26 Jesus is not simply returning the question, but is actually answering the lawyer by responding, in essence, "The answer to that is found in what you read of the Law every week in worship. What is that you recite?" This would point the lawyer back to the *Shema* (Deut. 6:5), which he recited in verse 27. The lawyer combines this with Leviticus 19:18, which stresses the love of one's neighbor. This combination of texts is found in at least one other rabbinic source, indicating it may have been a common way of summarizing the Law.

10:28 Jesus commends the answer. To live in love is the whole meaning of life in the kingdom of God.

10:29 The lawyer senses that he is being tested rather than Jesus (v. 25)! In an attempt to regain the initiative and transform this encounter into a debate about what the Law means by "neighbor," he asks Jesus another question. Given the understanding of "neighbor" at the time, his follow-up question was perfectly natural. For instance, the Pharisees assumed only other Pharisees were their neighbors, while other sects within Judaism taught that only members of their particular sect were neighbors. Jesus has already pointed out the superficiality of such an interpretation (Luke 6:27–36).

10:30 *going down.* This "was a notoriously dangerous road ... of narrow, rocky defiles, and of sudden turnings which made it the happy hunting ground of brigands" (Barclay). Roving gangs would ambush people sometimes by having one gang member pretend to be injured.

They stripped him. This detail is important. Since various ethnic groups wore distinctive clothing, it would now be impossible to tell whether the man was a Jew or not.

10:31 *A priest.* This priest may have been returning home after his period of temple service since Jericho was a principal area where priests lived when not on duty. There are at least two religious reasons why he may have passed by: (1) He could have thought the man was a sinner; if he helped him he would be working against his just punishment from God; (2) As a priest, he would not want to defile himself by touching a Gentile or a dead man (or even getting within about six feet of the man). Such defilement would be a humiliation after just completing his service at the temple. Defilement was seen as a threat to one's own spiritual condition. The priest's rule-book approach to spiritual life offered him several compelling reasons why he should simply pass by. He could even consider that he was honoring God by doing so.

10:32 *a Levite.* These were men assigned to aid the priests in various temple duties. Levites were not under the same regulations that guided the priests, and it appears he may have stopped and looked at the wounded man, perhaps speaking to him. Since he could not identify the man as a neighbor (i.e., a Jew) he, like the priest, decided not to get involved.

10:33 *a Samaritan.* The introduction of this character would have caught the audience off guard. Typically, when a person wanted to contrast the preoccupation of the religious elite over the details of the Law with the "common sense" piety of the average person, the progression would be between "a priest, a Levite, and a Jew," all of whom would have been returning home from service at the temple. Because this was such a stock formula in Jesus' day, the audience would have anticipated that the third man on the scene would be a Jewish layman who would do the right thing. Instead, Jesus invites the scorn of his listeners by this radical alteration of the formula by introducing a "good" Samaritan into the story. It would be like telling the story of "The Good Palestinian" to present-day Jews in Israel or the story of "The Good Apache" to residents of a western U.S. town in the 1800s. By making a hero out of a despised person, Jesus puts his Jewish audience in an awkward position: as they consider where they fit in the story, they don't want to identify with the priest and Levite (who showed such callousness), but are they willing to identify with a Samaritan? While priests and Levites had distinguished places in Jewish society, Samaritans were despised as half-breeds who had blended the worship of God with pagan practices. This term was used as an insult to describe a Jew who did not pay strict enough attention to religious tradition (John 8:48). While the roots of this prejudice reached back to the conquest of the northern kingdom of Israel by the Assyrians in 722 B.C., this ancient animosity was fresh in Jesus' day because some Samaritans had recently defiled the temple in Jerusalem by scattering bones in it.

took pity on him. Unlike the priest and Levite, the Samaritan was moved by compassion and stopped to help. Of all the characters in the story so far, he would have the least reason to suspect that the wounded man was his neighbor (i.e., a fellow Samaritan). Nevertheless, he helped him simply because he was a man in need.

10:34 *took him to an inn.* The nearest inn would be in Jericho, a place where Samaritans would be unwelcome. For the Samaritan to be willing to be identified was an act of love and courage, since the Jews in the community around the inn would assume that the Samaritan was somehow responsible for the injury to their tribesman.

10:35 *two silver coins.* Literally, this is two denarii, enough to care for the man for three weeks. The Samaritan also promised to reimburse whatever else it might cost to care for the man. Whereas the robbers beat, robbed and left the man, the Samaritan bound up his wounds, brought him to safety and promised to return.

10:36–39 *Which ... was a neighbor?* Jesus rephrases the lawyer's question (v. 29), and points out to him that he should act at least as generously and neighborly as this Samaritan (who had absolutely no ethnic or social obligation to the wounded man). "The question is not, 'Who is my neighbor?' but 'Am I being a neighbor to those needy ones whom the Lord places in my path?' " (Hendriksen). It is such sacrificial, generous and reckless love that is the evidence of truly loving God and others, and thus of the assurance of eternal life (v. 25).

UNIT 6—Parable of the Rich Fool / Luke 12:13–21

The Parable of the Rich Fool

¹³Someone in the crowd said to him, "Teacher, tell my brother to divide the inheritance with me."

¹⁴Jesus replied, "Man, who appointed me a judge or an arbiter between you?" ¹⁵Then he said to them, "Watch out! Be on your guard against all kinds of greed; a man's life does not consist in the abundance of his possessions."

¹⁶And he told them this parable: "The ground of a certain rich man produced a good crop. ¹⁷He thought to himself, 'What shall I do? I have no place to store my crops.'

¹⁸"Then he said, 'This is what I'll do. I will tear down my barns and build bigger ones, and there I will store all my grain and my goods. ¹⁹And I'll say to myself, "You have plenty of good things laid up for many years. Take life easy; eat, drink and be merry." '

²⁰"But God said to him, 'You fool! This very night your life will be demanded from you. Then who will get what you have prepared for yourself?'

²¹"This is how it will be with anyone who stores up things for himself but is not rich toward God."

READ

First Reading / First Impressions: If the rich man in this parable lived and died in our day, how would the local newspaper describe him in the obituaries?

- ❑ a tireless worker
- ❑ a success story
- ❑ foolish
- ❑ enterprising

Second Reading / Big Idea: What would you say is Jesus' theme in this parable?

SEARCH

1. What is likely going on behind the scenes that prompted the man's request (v. 13, see notes)?

2. Supposing that the man had a legitimate complaint, why does Jesus respond as he does (vv. 14–15)?

3. Jewish tradition viewed wealth as a gift from God to be used for the good of others. In light of that, how might Jesus' listeners have responded when they heard of the man's plan (vv. 18–19; see notes)?

Leadership Training Supplement

YOU ARE HERE

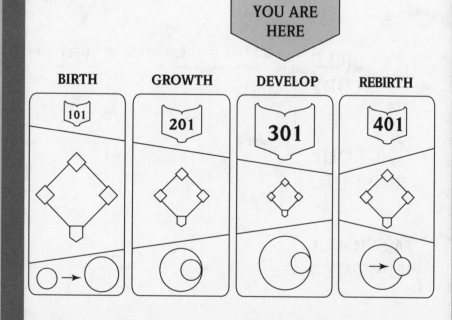

BIRTH	GROWTH	DEVELOP	REBIRTH
101	201	301	401

What is the game plan for your group in the 301 stage?

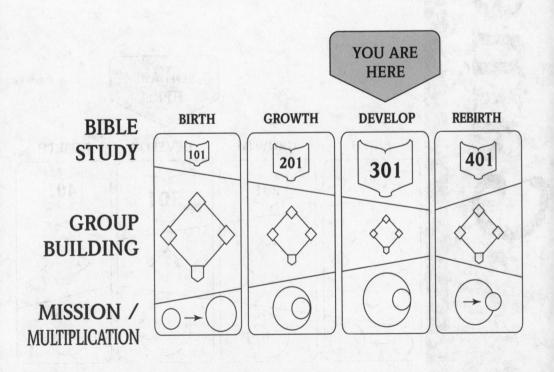

YOU ARE HERE

	BIRTH	GROWTH	DEVELOP	REBIRTH
BIBLE STUDY	101	201	301	401
GROUP BUILDING				
MISSION / MULTIPLICATION				

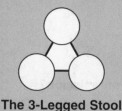

The 3-Legged Stool

The three essentials in a healthy small group are Bible Study, Group Building, and Mission / Multiplication. You need all three to stay balanced—like a 3-legged stool.

- To focus only on Bible Study will lead to scholasticism.
- To focus only on Group Building will lead to narcissism.
- To focus only on Mission will lead to burnout.

You need a game plan for the life cycle of the group where all of these elements are present in a purpose-driven strategy.

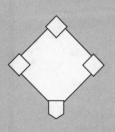

Bible Study

To develop the habit and skills for personal Bible Study.

TWO LEVELS: (1) Personal—on your own, and (2) Group study with your small group. In the personal Bible Study, you will be introduced to skills for reflection, self-inventory, creative writing and journaling.

Group Building

To move into discipleship with group accountability, shared leadership and depth community.

At the close of this course, the group building aspect will reach its goal by:

1. Facilitating intimate sharing
2. Developing accountability partners
3. Identifying and mentoring new leaders

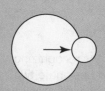

Mission / Multiplication

To prepare the members of the new leadership team from your group who are going to start a new group.

This Leadership Training Supplement is about your mission project. In six steps, your group will be led through a decision-making process to discover the new leadership team within your group who will prepare to form a new group in the Rebirth Stage.

Mission / Multiplication

Where are you in the 3-stage life cycle of your mission?

You can't sit on a one-legged stool—or even a two-legged stool. It takes all three. A Bible Study and Care Group that doesn't have a MISSION will fall.

Birthing Cycle

The mission is to begin the process of giving birth to a new group at the conclusion of this course. In this 301 course, you are supposed to be at stage three. If you are not at stage three, you can still reach the mission goal if you stay focused.

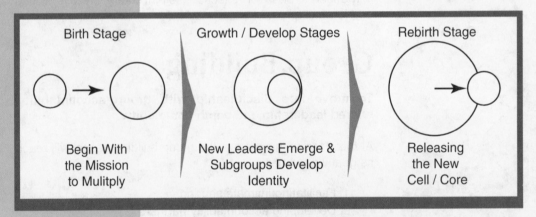

Birth Stage	Growth / Develop Stages	Rebirth Stage
Begin With the Mission to Mulitply	New Leaders Emerge & Subgroups Develop Identity	Releasing the New Cell / Core

The birthing process begins with DESIRE. If you do not want to birth a new group, it will never happen. Desire keeps the group focused on inviting new people into your group every week—until your group grows to about 12 or 15 people.

The second and third stage is PREGNANCY. By recognizing the gifts of people in your group, you are able to designate two or three people who will ultimately be the missionaries in your group to form a new group. This is called the "leadership core."

The fourth stage is REBIRTH—which takes place at the end of this course, when the whole group commissions the core or cell to move out and start the new group. Our 401 course "Rebirth" is a five-week journey to facilitate the Rebirth Process.

6 Steps to Birth a Group

Step 1   ## Desire

Is your group purpose-driven about mission?

Take this pop quiz and see how purpose-driven you are. Then, study the "four fallacies" about groups.

Step 2   ## Assessment

Is your church purpose-driven about groups?

Pinpoint where you are coming from and where most of the people in small groups in your church come from.

Step 3   ## Survey

Where's the itch for those in your church who are not involved in groups?

Take this churchwide survey to discover the felt needs of those in your church who do not seem to be interested in small groups.

Step 4   ## Brainstorming

What did you learn about your church from the survey?

Debrief the survey in the previous step to decide how your small group could make a difference in starting a new group.

Step 5   ## Barnstorming

Who are you going to invite?

Build a prospect list of people you think might be interested in joining a new group.

Step 6   ## Commissioning

Congratulations. You deserve a party.

Commission the leadership core from your group who are going to be your missionaries to start a new group. Then, for the rest of the "mother group," work on your covenant for starting over ... with a few empty chairs and rebuilding this group.

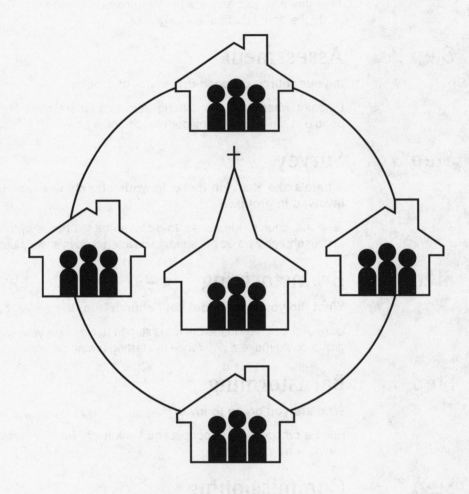

Step 1

Desire

Is your group purpose-driven about mission?

The greatest danger to any chain is its strongest link. This is especially true of Bible Study groups. The very depth of the study keeps new people from joining, or feeling comfortable when they join. In the end the group grows inward, becoming self-centered and spiritually insensitive.

To prevent this from happening in your group, take this pop quiz and share the results with your group.

	Yes	No
1. Are you a committed follower of Jesus Christ?	☐	☐
2. Do you believe that Jesus Christ wants you to share your faith with others?	☐	☐
3. Do you believe that every Christian needs to belong to a small, caring community where Jesus Christ is affirmed?	☐	☐
4. Do you know of people in your church who are not presently involved in a small group?	☐	☐
5. Do you know friends on the fringe of the church who need to belong to a life-sharing small group?	☐	☐
6. Do you believe that God has a will and plan for your life?	☐	☐
7. Are you willing to be open to what God might do through you in this small group?	☐	☐
8. Are you open to the possibility that God might use you to form a new group?	☐	☐

If you can't say "No" to any of these questions, consider yourself committed!

What Is a Small Group?

A Small Group is an intentional, face-to-face gathering of people in a similar stage of life at a regular time with a common purpose of discovering and growing in a relationship with Jesus Christ.

Small Groups are the disciple-making strategy of Flamingo Road Church. The behaviors of the 12-step strategy (to request information: www.flamingoroad.org) are the goals we want to achieve with each individual in a small group. These goals are accomplished through a new members class (membership) and continues in a regular ongoing small group (maturity, ministry and multiplication).

Keys to an Effective Small Group Ministry

1. Care for all people (members/guests) through organized active Care Groups.
2. Teach the Bible interactively while making life application.
3. Build a Servant Leadership Team.
4. Birth New Groups

Commitments of All Small Group Leaders Are ...

1. to model the behaviors represented in the 12-step strategy
2. to lead their group to be an effective small group as mentioned above
3. to use curriculum approved by small group pastor
4. to build a leadership team

Taken from the Small Group Training Manual of Flamingo Road Community Church, Fort Lauderdale, FL.

Four Fallacies About Small Groups

Are you suffering from one of these four misconceptions when it comes to small groups? Check yourself on these fallacies.

Fallacy #1: It takes 10 to 12 people to start a small group.

Wrong. The best size to start with is three or four people—which leaves room in the group for growth. Start "small" and pray that God will fill the "empty chair" ... and watch it happen.

Fallacy #2: It takes a lot of skill to lead a small group.

Wrong again. Sticking to the three-part tight agenda makes it possible for nearly anyone to lead a group. For certain support and recovery groups more skills are required, but the typical Bible Study and Care Group can be led by anyone with lots of heart and vision.

Fallacy #3: To assure confidentiality, the "door" should be closed after the first session.

For certain "high risk" groups this is true; but for the average Bible Study and Care Group all you need is the rule that "nothing that is said in the group is discussed outside of the group."

Fallacy #4: The longer the group lasts, the better it gets.

Not necessarily. The bell curve for effective small groups usually peaks in the second year. Unless new life is brought into the group, the group will decline in vitality. It is better to release the group (and become a reunion group) when it is at its peak than to run the risk of burnout.

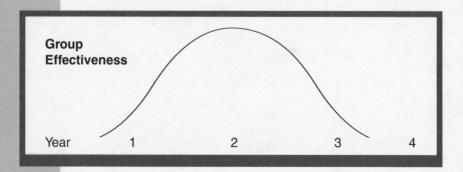

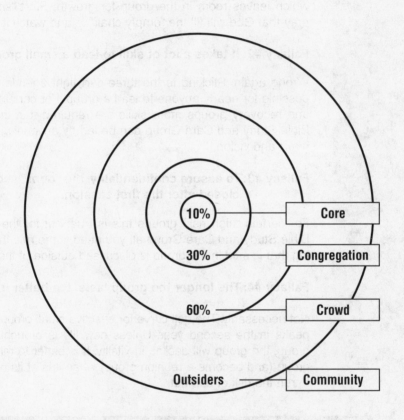

Step **2**

Assessment

Is your church purpose-driven about groups?

Most of the people who come to small groups in the church are from the highly committed CORE of the church. How about your group?

Pinpoint Your Group

The graph on the opposite page represents the four types of people typically found in your church and in your community.

- **10% Core:** The "spiritual core" of the church and the church leadership.

- **30% Congregation:** Those who come to church regularly and are faithful in giving.

- **60% Crowd:** Those on the membership roles who attend only twice a year. They have fallen through the cracks.

- **Outside Community:** Those who live in the surrounding area but do not belong to any church.

Step 1: On the opposite page, put a series of dots in the appropriate circles where the members of your group come from.

Step 2: If you know of other small groups in your church, put some more dots on the graph to represent the people in those groups. When you are finished, stop and ask your group this question:

"Why do the groups in our church appeal only to the people who are represented by the dots on this graph?"

Four Kinds of Small Groups

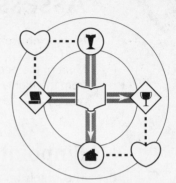

FELT NEED / RECOVERY GROUPS
- Felt needs
- Short-term
- Low-level commitment
- Seeker Bible Study

These groups are designed to appeal to hurting people on the fringe of the church and in the community.

PULPIT-BASED GROUPS
- Around the Scripture in the Sunday lesson
- With handout in Sunday bulletin
- With discussion questions
- No homework

These groups are designed to appeal to those who come to church and listen to the sermon but do not want to do homework.

DISCIPLESHIP / DEPTH BIBLE STUDY GROUPS
- Year-long commitment
- Depth Bible Study
- Homework option
- Curriculum based

These groups are designed to appeal to the 10% highly committed core of the church who are ready for discipleship.

COVENANT OR NURTURE GROUPS
- Four-stage life cycle
- Renewal option
- Begins with 7-week contract
- Graded levels of Bible Study: 101, 201 and 301

Church Evaluation

You do NOT have to complete this assessment if you are not in the leadership core of your church, but it would be extremely valuable if your group does have members in the leadership core of your church.

1. Currently, what percentage of your church members are involved in small groups?

2. What kind of small groups are you offering in your church? (Study the four kinds of groups on the opposite page.)
   ❐ Felt Need / Recovery Groups
   ❐ Pulpit-Based Groups
   ❐ Discipleship / Depth Bible Study Groups
   ❐ Four-stage Covenant or Nurture Groups

3. Which statement below represents the position of your church on small groups?
   ❐ "Small Groups have never been on the drawing board at our church."
   ❐ "We have had small groups, but they fizzled."
   ❐ "Our church leadership has had negative experiences with small groups."
   ❐ "Small groups are the hope for our future."
   ❐ "We have Sunday school; that's plenty."

4. How would you describe the people who usually get involved in small groups?
   ❐ 10% Core   ❐ 30% Congregation   ❐ 60% Crowd

Risk and Supervision
This depends on the risk level of the group—the higher the risk, the higher the supervision. For the typical Bible Study group ⬠ , pulpit-based group (Y), or covenant group ◆ (where there is little risk), supervision is minimal. For some support groups ♡ and all recovery groups ⚡ , training and supervision are required.

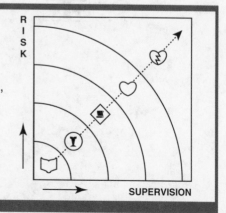

Step 3 Survey

Where's the itch for those in your church who are not involved in groups?

This survey has been written for churchwide use—in hopes that you may be able to rewrite it and use it in your own church. The courses described in this survey are taken from the present Serendipity courses for small groups.

CHURCHWIDE SURVEY

Name_____ Phone_____

1. Which of these shared-experience groups might be of interest to you? Check all that apply in the grid below under question 1 (Q1).

2. Which of these shared-experience groups would you be interested in hosting or co-leading? Check all that apply in the grid below under question 2 (Q2).

3. Which of these shared-experience groups do you think would be of interest to a friend or relative of yours who is on the fringe of the church? Check all that apply in the grid below under question 3 (Q3).

FELT NEED Electives — 7- to 13-week groups

	Q1	Q2	Q3
1. Dealing With Grief & Loss (Hope in the Midst of Pain)	☐	☐	☐
2. Divorce Recovery (Picking Up the Pieces)	☐	☐	☐
3. Marriage Enrichment (Making a Good Marriage Better)	☐	☐	☐
4. Parenting Adolescents (Easing the Way to Adulthood)	☐	☐	☐
5. Healthy Relationships (Living Within Defined Boundaries)	☐	☐	☐
6. Stress Management (Finding the Balance)	☐	☐	☐
7. 12 Steps (The Path to Wholeness)	☐	☐	☐
8. Blended Families (Yours, Mine, Ours)	☐	☐	☐

BEGINNER Electives — 7- to 13-week groups

	Q1	Q2	Q3
9. Stressed Out (Keeping Your Cool)	☐	☐	☐
10. Core Values (Setting My Moral Compass)	☐	☐	☐

	Q1	Q2	Q3
11. Marriage (Seasons of Growth)	☐	☐	☐
12. Jesus (Up Close & Personal)	☐	☐	☐
13. Gifts & Calling (Discovering God's Will)	☐	☐	☐
14. Relationships (Learning to Love)	☐	☐	☐
15. Assessment (Personal Audit)	☐	☐	☐
16. Family (Stages of Parenting)	☐	☐	☐
17. Wholeness (Time for a Checkup)	☐	☐	☐
18. Beliefs (Basic Christianity)	☐	☐	☐
19. Men of Faith	☐	☐	☐
20. Women of Faith	☐	☐	☐

DEEPER Bible Study — Varying Length Courses

	Q1	Q2	Q3
21. Supernatural: Amazing Stories (Jesus' Miracles)	☐	☐	☐
22. Discipleship: In His Steps (Life of Christ)	☐	☐	☐
23. Wisdom: The Jesus Classics (Jesus' Parables)	☐	☐	☐
24. Challenge: Attitude Adjustment (Sermon on the Mount)	☐	☐	☐
25. Endurance: Running the Race (Philippians)	☐	☐	☐
26. Teamwork: Together in Christ (Ephesians)	☐	☐	☐
27. Integrity: Taking on Tough Issues (1 Corinthians)	☐	☐	☐
28. Gospel: Jesus of Nazareth (Gospel of Mark)	☐	☐	☐
29. Leadership: Passing the Torch (1 & 2 Timothy)	☐	☐	☐
30. Excellence: Mastering the Basics (Romans)	☐	☐	☐
31. Hope: Looking at the End of Time (Revelation)	☐	☐	☐
32. Faithfulness: Walking in the Light (1 John)	☐	☐	☐
33. Freedom: Living by Grace (Galatians)	☐	☐	☐
34. Perseverance: Staying the Course (1 Peter)	☐	☐	☐
35. Performance: Faith at Work (James)	☐	☐	☐

DEPTH Bible Study — 13-week groups

	Q1	Q2	Q3
36. Ephesians (Our Riches in Christ)	☐	☐	☐
37. James (Walking the Talk)	☐	☐	☐
38. Life of Christ (Behold the Man)	☐	☐	☐
39. Miracles (Signs and Wonders)	☐	☐	☐
40. Parables (Virtual Reality)	☐	☐	☐
41. Philippians (Joy Under Stress)	☐	☐	☐
42. Sermon on the Mount (Examining Your Life)	☐	☐	☐
43. 1 John (The Test of Faith)	☐	☐	☐

Section 2: Covenant Groups (Long-term)

A covenant group is longer term (like an extended family), starting with a commitment for 7–13 weeks, with an option of renewing your covenant for the rest of the year. A covenant group can decide to change the topics they study over time. The general themes for the covenant groups that our church is considering are listed on the previous two pages.

4. Which of the following long-term covenant groups would you be interested in?

- ❒ Singles
- ❒ Couples
- ❒ Twenty-Something
- ❒ Mixed
- ❒ Young Marrieds

- ❒ Men
- ❒ Parents
- ❒ Thirty-Something
- ❒ Breakfast
- ❒ Seniors

- ❒ Women
- ❒ Downtown
- ❒ Empty Nesters
- ❒ Engineers
- ❒ Sunday Brunch

Section 3: Pre-Covenant Groups (Short-term)

To give you a taste of a small group, our church is offering a 7-week "trial" program for groups. For this trial program, the group will use the course **Beginnings: A Taste of Serendipity.**

5. Would you be interested in joining a "trial" group?

- ❒ Yes
- ❒ No
- ❒ Maybe

6. What would be the most convenient time and place for you to meet?

- ❒ Weekday morning
- ❒ Weekday evening
- ❒ Saturday morning
- ❒ Sunday after church

- ❒ At church
- ❒ In a home

7. What kind of group would you prefer?

- ❒ Men
- ❒ Women
- ❒ Singles
- ❒ Couples
- ❒ Mixed
- ❒ Parents
- ❒ Seniors
- ❒ Around my age
- ❒ Doesn't matter

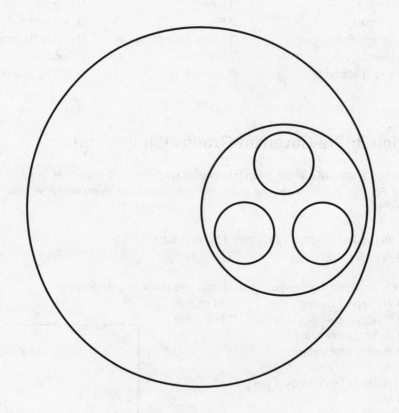

Step 4 Brainstorming

What did you learn about your church from the survey?

The Itch: Debrief together what you discovered from the survey about the need for small groups in your church. To begin with, find out in your group who checked Q3 for any courses 1–20. Jot down in the box below the top three courses that you checked for 1–20.

Top Three Courses:

The Nitch: For the top three courses in the box above, find out if anyone in your group checked Q2 for these courses—i.e., that they would be willing to host or help lead a group that was interested in this course. Jot down the names of those in your group who checked Q2 in the box below.

Potential Hosts and Leaders:

The Apprentice / Leader and Leadership Core: Now, as a group, look over the names of the potential hosts and leaders you put in the box above and try to discern the person on this list who you think could easily be the leader of this new group, and one or two others who might fill out the Leadership Core for this new group. Jot down these names in the box below.

Apprentice / Leader and Leadership Core:

Q&A

What is the purpose of Covenant Groups?*

The members of the Covenant Group come together for the purpose of helping each other to:

- *Love God with all their heart, soul, mind and strength (Mark 12:30).*
- *Love their neighbors as themselves (Mark 12:31).*
- *Make disciples (Matthew 28:19).*

What are the qualifications of a Covenant Group leader?

A Covenant Group leader functions as a lay pastor, taking on himself or herself the responsibility of providing the primary care for the members of the group. Therefore, a Covenant Group leader exemplifies the following characteristics:

- *believes in Jesus Christ as their Lord and Savior*
- *has been a Christian for a while*
- *continues to grow in their faith*
- *cares for the well-being of others*
- *is able to set goals and work toward them*
- *demonstrates moral integrity*
- *listens to others*
- *is empathetic*
- *is willing to learn from others*
- *demonstrates flexibility*
- *respects others*
- *senses a call to serve*

A Covenant Group leader is not a perfect person! He or she need not know everything about leading and caring for others. Skills valuable to the role of a leader will be taught throughout the year, and care for the leader will be provided on an ongoing basis through a coach.

A Covenant Group leader is not necessarily a teacher. It is far more important that the leader be able to shepherd and care for the others in the group. Teaching is often a shared responsibility among group members.

---

* These four pages (M20–M23) are taken from the Training Manual For Group Leaders at Zionsville Presbyterian Church, Zionsville, IN, and are used by permission.

Questions & Answers

What does the church expect of a Covenant Group leader?

Every leader is asked to agree to the terms of the leader's covenant. Covenant Group leaders are to attend the monthly STP (Sharing, Training and Prayer) meeting. This gathering is held for the purposes of training and supporting leaders. The meeting takes place on the third Tuesday of each month, from 6:45 p.m. to 8:30 p.m. The two main elements of the STP event concern communication. The first half of the evening is devoted to disseminating the vision. The second half of the meeting consists of leaders huddling with their coach and with each other for the purpose of learning from one another. If a leader is unable to attend this meeting for some significant reason, he or she is to arrange another time to meet with their coach.

Leaders are also to fill out the Group Leader's Summary after every group event. This one-page reporting form takes only 10 minutes or so to complete and is a vital communication link between the staff liaison, the coach and the leader.

What can a Covenant Group leader expect in the way of support from the church?

A Covenant Group leader can expect the session and the staff to hold to the terms laid out in the Church's Covenant.

Every leader will be given a coach. This coach is someone whose ministry is to care for up to five leaders. The coach is charged with the responsibility of resourcing, encouraging, supporting, evaluating, challenging, loving and listening to the leaders in his or her care.

Every coach is supported by a staff member. If leaders ever have a situation where they feel that their coach is unable to help them, the staff liaison is there to be of assistance.

What is the role of a Covenant Group leader?

When people come together in groups, the group itself becomes an entity that is greater than the sum of its parts. The Covenant Group leader watches over the life and health of this new entity.

Specifically the Covenant Group leader is to:

- *find an apprentice*
- *pray and prepare for group meetings*
- *notify their coach or staff of acute crisis conditions requiring response*
- *develop and maintain an atmosphere in which members of the group can discover and develop God-given spiritual gifts*
- *pray for the spiritual growth and protection of each member*
- *refer counseling cases that exceed experience level*
- *convene the group two to four times each month*
- *recruit a host/hostess, when appropriate, and to see that child care and refreshments are available and a venue is arranged*
- *develop a healthy balance of love, learn, do, decide*
- *assure God's redemptive agenda via Scripture, sharing, prayers, songs and worship*
- *assist the group in refraining from divisiveness or teachings contrary to church position*
- *accept responsibility for group growth through the open-chair strategy*
- *lead an exemplary life*
- *regularly touch base with members outside the context of the group meeting just to say "Hi" and to see how they are doing*
- *help the group form a covenant and to review the covenant periodically*

While the Covenant Group leader takes primary responsibility for these activities, he or she should involve members of the group in many of them.

Does a Covenant Group really have to have a leader?

Yes! Without a leader a Covenant Group is like a ship at sea with no captain. A ship without a captain is at the mercy of the prevailing current and is unable to prepare for what may lie ahead. However, a ship with a captain has her course mapped out, and there is always someone at the helm ready to respond if necessary. So it is with a Covenant Group. The leader serves the others in the group by working to chart the best course as they together pursue being God's people on earth.

Questions & Answers

What are the critical elements of a Covenant Group?

A Covenant Group needs to have:

- *a leader*
- *an apprentice / leader*
- *members*
- *an open chair*
- *a covenant (see page M32)*

What is an Apprentice / Leader and how do we find one?

An apprentice / leader is someone who agrees that in time he or she will step out into leadership. Historically churches have tended to ask only those who aggressively step forward to serve in leadership positions. Rarely have churches worked at developing leaders. The result has been that most churches experience the phenomenon where only 20% of the congregation does 80% of the work. This historical approach stifles the giftedness of 80% of the church's population! In addition, the church has burned out many of their stand-out leaders by asking them to lead too many programs and too many people. Without some form of apprentice / leadership development, the church is constrained to overload its highly motivated, "here-I-am-send-me" leaders. The apprentice / leader model is meant to address these concerns.

The apprentice / leader is not an assistant. An assistant seldom has plans of stepping into the leader's shoes. Instead, the apprentice / leader works alongside the leader, with the intent of one day becoming a leader themselves. Along the way he or she is experiencing on-the-job training, learning the skills necessary to serve a small group as its leader.

It is the responsibility of the leader to find an apprentice / leader. The most important tools for the leader in this process are prayer and observation. The leader should pray, asking God to send someone whom he or she could mentor and train as a leader. Accompanying these prayers should be efforts to observe those who demonstrate signs of giftedness in shepherding, organizing, listening and faith. The one who is on time and who routinely prepares diligently for the group could be a candidate. The leader could also begin using the time before and after worship services, as well as various fellowship and educational events, to meet others in the congregation. As relationships are established, and the extent of a leader's acquaintances are broadened, the opportunity for finding a suitable apprentice / leader increases.

Leadership Training

Step 5 Barnstorming

Who are you going to invite?

In the previous step, you identified the Apprentice / Leader and one or two others in your group who are going to be the leadership cell or core to start a new group.

Now, as a whole group, spend a few minutes creating a prospect list of people you would like to invite into this new group. Ask someone in your group to be the secretary and write down in the boxes below the names of people who come to mind:

Friends: Who are your friends in the church who you think might be interested in a small group?

Affinity: What are the special interests of the people in your leadership cell and who are the people in your church with the same interests? For instance, if the people in your leadership cell love tennis, who are the people in your church who might be interested in a small group before tennis? What about book lovers, entrepreneurs, empty nesters, senior citizens, stock watchers, etc.?

How Serendipity 101 Courses
Make Leading A Beginner Group Easy:

1. *Each session has get acquainted* **Ice-Breakers** *to get your group started and a* **3-Part Tight Agenda** *to keep it on track!*

2. **Two Options** *for breaking open the Word:*
- **Option 1: Light**—*for people who are not familiar with the Bible*
- **Option 2: Heavy**—*for people who are familiar with the Bible*

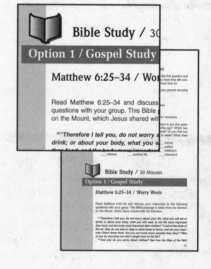

3. **Study Helps** *for the Group Leader include Margin Tips, Reference Notes and Guided Questionnaires for Bible Study.*

Felt Needs: Who are the people you know with the same felt needs? These people might be on the fringe of the church or even outside of the church. Go back to the survey on pages M15–M16 (the 101 courses) and think of people you feel could be hot prospects. For instance, who would be interested in "Stressed Out," "Marriage," "Wholeness," "Healthy Relationships," "Parenting Adolescents," etc.?

Geographical Location: Where do the people in your leadership team live or work, and who are the people in your church in the same area?

The Four Circles: Now, on this diagram, pinpoint the people you have jotted down in the four circles. Do you have any people on this list from the **Crowd** (the church dropouts)? Do you have anyone on your list from the **Community** (who do not attend any church)? It's really important that you have people from all four circles on your list.

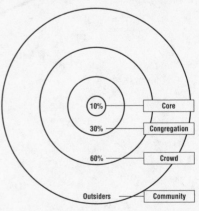

Step 6 Commissioning

Congratulations. You deserve a party.

Only two things remain for you to decide: (1) How are you going to commission the leadership team for the new group and (2) What is the rest of your group going to do next?

Going-away party

You have several options. If the church is planning a church-wide event for all of the groups (such as a graduation banquet), you would have a table at this event for your group. If your church is not planning an event, you must plan your own going-away party.

At this party, you may want to reminisce about your life together as a group with the questions below, have fun making some "Wild Predictions" (see page M30), share a Bible Study time (see page M31), and conclude with a time of commissioning and prayer.

Reminiscing Questions

1. What do you remember about the first time you attended this group?

2. How did you feel about opening up in this group and sharing your story?

3. What was the funniest thing that happened in this group?

4. What was the high point for you in this group?

5. What will you miss most about this group?

6. How would you like this group to stay in touch with each other after you multiply?

7. How did this group contribute to your life?

8. What is the biggest change that has occurred in your life since joining this group?

Wild Predictions

Try to match the people in your group to the crazy forecasts below. (Don't take it too seriously; it's meant to be fun!) Read out loud the first item and ask everyone to call out the name of the person who is most likely to accomplish this feat. Then, read the next item and ask everyone to make a new prediction, etc.

THE PERSON IN OUR GROUP MOST LIKELY TO ...

Make a million selling Beanie Babies over the Internet

Become famous for designing new attire for sumo wrestlers

Replace Vanna White on *Wheel of Fortune*

Appear on *The Tonight Show* to exhibit an acrobatic talent

Move to a desert island

Discover a new use for underarm deodorant

Succeed David Letterman as host of *The Late Show*

Substitute for John Madden as Fox's football color analyst

Appear on the cover of *Muscle & Fitness Magazine*

Become the newest member of the Spice Girls

Work as a bodyguard for Rush Limbaugh at Feminist convention

Write a best-selling novel based on their love life

Be a dance instructor on a cruise ship for wealthy, well-endowed widows

Win the blue ribbon at the state fair for best Rocky Mountain oyster recipe

Land a job as head librarian for Amazon.com

Be the first woman to win the Indianapolis 500

Open the Clouseau Private Detective Agency

Going-Away Party

Reflection Bible Study

Barnabas and Saul Sent Off — Acts 13:1–3, NIV

13 *In the church at Antioch there were prophets and teachers: Barnabas, Simeon called Niger, Lucius of Cyrene, Manaen (who had been brought up with Herod the tetrarch) and Saul. ²While they were worshiping the Lord and fasting, the Holy Spirit said, "Set apart for me Barnabas and Saul for the work to which I have called them."³So after they had fasted and prayed, they placed their hands on them and sent them off.*

1. Why do you think God chose this small group in Antioch to launch the first missionary journey (instead of the church headquarters in Jerusalem)?
   - ❏ It was merely coincidental.
   - ☑ They were following the leading of the Holy Spirit.
   - ❏ They were a bunch of outcasts from the fringe of the church.
   - ❏ They didn't know how to "paint inside the lines."

2. How do you think the leadership back in Jerusalem felt when they heard what these guys were doing?
   - ❏ thrilled
   - ❏ embarrassed
   - ❏ angry that they didn't follow protocol
   - ☑ They probably didn't hear about it until later.

3. Why do you think the small group chose two people to send out instead of one?
   - ❏ for companionship
   - ☑ They had different gifts: Paul was a hothead, Barnabas an encourager.
   - ❏ It was coincidental.

4. As you think about sending out some members of your small group to give "birth" to a new group, what is your greatest concern for these people?
   - ☑ keeping the faith
   - ❏ keeping the vision
   - ❏ keeping their personal walk with Christ
   - ❏ keeping in touch with us for support

5. As one who is going to lead or colead a new group, how would you describe your emotions right now?
   - ❏ a nervous wreck
   - ❏ pregnant with excitement
   - ☑ delivery room jitters
   - ❏ Ask me next week.

6. If you could say one word of encouragement to those who are going to be new leaders, what would it be?
   - ☑ I'll be praying for you.
   - ❏ Call me anytime.
   - ❏ You can do it.
   - ❏ It's okay to fail.

What do we do next?

For those who are going to stay with the "mother group," you need to decide on your new covenant and who you are going to invite to fill the empty chairs left by the departing "missionaries."

Do we ever meet again?

Definitely! Plan NOW for "homecoming" next year when the new group returns for a time of celebration. Four good times: the World Series, Super Bowl, Final Four and Stanley Cup.

Group Covenant

Any group can benefit from creating or renewing a group covenant. Take some time for those remaining in the "mother group" to discuss the following questions. When everyone in the group has the same expectations for the group, everything runs more smoothly.

1. The purpose of our group is:

2. The goals of our group are:

3. We will meet on _____ (day of week)

4. We will meet for _____ weeks, after which we will decide if we wish to continue as a group. If we do decide to continue, we will reconsider this covenant.

5. We will meet _____ (weekly, every other week, monthly).

6. Our meetings will be from _____ o'clock to _____ o'clock, and we will strive to start and end on time.

7. We will meet at _____ or rotate from house to house.

8. We will take care of the following details: ❏ child care   ❏ refreshments

9. We agree to the following rules for our group:

   ❏ PRIORITY: While you are in this course of study, you give the group meetings priority.

   ❏ PARTICIPATION: Everyone is encouraged to participate and no one dominates.

   ❏ RESPECT: Everyone is given the right to his or her own opinion, and all questions are encouraged and respected.

   ❏ CONFIDENTIALITY: Anything that is said in the meeting is never repeated outside the meeting.

   ❏ LIFE CHANGE: We will regularly assess our own life change goals and encourage one another in our pursuit of Christlikeness.

   ❏ EMPTY CHAIR: The group stays open to reaching new people at every meeting.

   ❏ CARE & SUPPORT: Permission is given to call upon each other at any time especially in times of crisis. The group will provide care for every member.

   ❏ ACCOUNTABILITY: We agree to let the members of the group hold us accountable to the commitments which each of us make in whatever loving ways we decide upon.

   ❏ MISSION: We will do everything in our power to start a new group.

   ❏ MINISTRY: The group will encourage one another to volunteer and serve in a ministry, and to support missions by giving financially and/or personally serving.

4. What was it about the man's attitude that led to his condemnation from God (see note on v. 20)?

5. From verse 21, what does Jesus mean by being "rich toward God" (see note)?

6. Suppose two people each receive a large, unexpected inheritance. One wants to develop an investment portfolio guaranteeing financial freedom for the rest of his life, while the other wants to invest
in becoming rich toward God. What are some of the differences you would expect to see in each
regarding the way they ...

pray:

view the needs of others around them:

deal with their families' needs for food, shelter, education, etc.:

evaluate what makes for a wise investment:

make political and social decisions:

APPLY

1. If you should die tonight, what could be said about you in the obituaries? Fill in the blanks below:
   - Last night, _____ died suddenly.
   - He/She will always be remembered for_____.
   - He/She always had time for _____.
   - He/She felt that possessions were _____

2. Is it possible for you to have a drive to accumulate wealth, and also to be "rich toward God"? If so,
how? If not, why not?

3. Jesus warned us that "a man's life does not consist in the abundance of his possessions" (v. 15).
How does this warning apply to you?
   - ❐ Ouch! I may be blowing it.   ❐ I'm not sure I understand.
   - ❐ It's a good reminder.   ❐ I'm working to find the right balance.
   - ❐ I know this is true, and I'm working on my priorities. ❐ other:_____

GROUP AGENDA

After the first part, read the Scripture out loud and divide into groups of 4. Then come back together for the third part.

TO BEGIN / 10–15 Min. (Choose 1 or 2)
1. If your home caught on fire and your family and pets were safe, what three possessions would you try to rescue?

2. If you suddenly received a large sum of money, what would you do with it?

3. Who do you admire for their attitude toward money and material things?

TO GO DEEPER / 30 Min. (Choose 2 or 3)
1. Regarding this passage, what stands out to you from the READ and SEARCH questions or the study notes?

2. What is Jesus' position in this parable on money? What would Jesus say about our view of money, especially the "American Dream" of success?

3. "Take life easy; eat, drink and be merry." How attractive is that philosophy of life to you?

4. How do you balance the message of this parable with Scripture that teaches the need to provide for your family (e.g. 1 Tim. 5:8)?

5. What does an investment portfolio guided by a desire to be rich toward God contain in areas like savings, retirement, and estate planning? How are you handling these issues?

6. CASE STUDY: Walter grew up in a nice middle-class home in the suburbs, went to college, and married his sweetheart. Their first child is on the way and Walter's wife will have to take a leave of absence from her work, leaving them to cope with Walter's schoolteacher's salary. All of their dreams about having a nice home are dashed. Should he seek other employment or should they cut back on their lifestyle?

TO CLOSE / 15–30 Min.
1. Are you thinking and dreaming about your group's mission? (See the center section.)

2. How did you feel about your answers to the questions in APPLY? If your life ended "this very night," what would be your biggest regret? What can you do now to change that?

3. How would you like the group to pray for you?

NOTES

Summary. Whereas the preceding section (Luke 12:1–12) warned the disciples to "be on your guard" against the danger of hypocrisy, this parable warns them to "watch out" (v. 15) for the danger of placing top priority on the concern for material wealth.

12:13 *Teacher.* Literally, this is "Rabbi." As men schooled in the Law of God, rabbis were often asked to settle legal disputes.

divide the inheritance. When a father died, he would bequeath his estate to his sons in the hope that they might keep the property together. However, if the sons could not "live together in unity" (Ps. 133:1), one could sue for the property to be legally divided. Apparently this man and his brother disagreed about if (or how) such a division should be made.

12:14 *Man.* This is akin to someone today saying, "Listen, mister ... ." Jesus is clearly rebuking the man for his request.

who appointed me a judge ... between you? Jesus refuses to be used as a pawn for this man's material gain. Instead of being drawn into siding with him as a judge against his brother, Jesus effectively becomes the judge over both of them, exposing the motivation of their hearts. While the man claimed to simply want justice, his vision of justice was more tied up with gaining his share of material possessions than it was with pursuing reconciliation with an estranged brother. The use of "justice" as a cloak for material gain was of no interest to Jesus.

12:15 *greed.* Jesus pinpoints the real motivating factor behind this appeal for justice. Literally, the word means to "always thirst for more."

life. The Greek word used here (*zoe*) refers not simply to biological life, but to the quality of one's life. Then, as now, a person's happiness and well-being was often thought to be determined by what he or she owned. Jesus flatly rejects this as a standard for measuring the worth of one's life.

12:16–20 This parable illustrates the principle of verse 15. Verses 16–17 raise the problem the man faces.

12:16 *The ground.* The Greek word here, *chora*, implies "extensive holdings, normally a district or region" (Stott). The use of this word accentuates the extent of the man's wealth. The fact that this crop was produced by the man's land indicates that the crop was a gift to him. It was not something he particularly earned or deserved. He simply inherited the lavish abundance of a God-given crop.

a good crop. This word is used only here in the New Testament. In the Greek, there is a play on words as the parable develops. The man has an *euphoreo* ("good crop") which he thinks will lead to *euphron* ("the enjoyment of the good life"—v. 19), yet God calls him an *aphron* ("a fool"—v. 20).

12:18–19 The man's solution for his problem of overabundance was simply to store up his possessions so he could relax, feast and party.

12:18 *tear down ... and build.* Since he is already a rich man prior to this particular harvest, one would assume he already has a large amount of storage capacity. The need (and resources!) to build new buildings accents the miraculous nature of this harvest.

there I will store all my grain and my goods. Up to this point in the story, the listeners would view the man as blessed by God. Even his plan to store the crop for future use could be commended, since the story reverberates with the centuries-old account of how Joseph stored up the abundant crops of Egypt for seven years, so that when the time of famine came he would have resources with which to provide for his people (Gen. 41:33–57). It would be right for this man, blessed by God with this miraculous crop, to store it as God's merciful provision for the people when hard times came upon them. The problem, already hinted at in this verse, is that the man sees it as "my grain and my goods."

12:19 *eat, drink and be merry.* This was a stock phrase from popular caricatures of Epicurean philosophy, which placed the ultimate priority on human pleasure (see also Isa. 22:12–14; 1 Cor. 15:32). Jewish ethics had little respect for this approach to life, since it failed to acknowledge one's responsibility to God and others. It is significant that while the stock phrase ends with "... for tomorrow we die," this man thought that by means of his abundant possessions he might be able to enjoy a life of self-indulgent pleasure for years to come. At this point in the story, the listeners would realize things were going terribly wrong. The man was not following the ways of God, but living as a pagan, concerned only with his own desires. Jewish ethics would echo what Paul makes clear in his letters regarding the purpose of work: first, one is to provide for one's own needs and that of one's family (2 Thess. 3:7–12), and, secondly, one is to give to those in need (Eph. 4:28). This man had

ample provision for his own needs. Therefore, he should have found storage for the surplus in "the bosoms of the needy, the houses of widows, the mouths of orphans and of infants" (Trench). Instead, he hoards the riches for himself. Failing to see his bumper crop as a gift from God to be shared with others, he sees it as his own possession to be used as he pleases. Ultimately, he also fails to see his life as a gift from God to whom he is responsible for how he lives (v. 20).

12:20 While the man has been the sole character in the story so far, the final word in the parable belongs to God. The ultimate reality of God's judgment shows that making a priority out of seeking wealth for one's own pleasure is meaningless.

You fool! In the Bible, a fool is someone who lives without regard to God.

your life will be demanded from you. The word for "demanded" is a word used in banking circles when a loan was being called in for payment. The man's life, like all his possessions, was a loan from God—to whom he is now accountable for its use.

who will get what you have prepared for yourself? This might be understood in two ways: (1) It points out the foolishness of living for material possessions, since at one's death they are of no use to the one who clung to them. He will not be the one to possess what he spent his life preparing to have! (2) It might have been intended to point out his isolation. Having chosen wealth as his god, he is alienated from friends or family. There is no one close to him to whom he can pass on an inheritance when he dies. Greed isolates people from true human relationships.

12:21 *This is how it will be.* Jesus applies the parable to his listeners. Those who are preoccupied with hoarding material provisions for themselves forfeit life with God and alienate themselves from their own families.

rich toward God. Literally, this is "gathering riches for God." Luke 12:33 reveals that one does this by making a priority of giving generously and lavishly to those in need. Disciples can freely give to others because they recognize that God is the provider of all they have and need. Therefore, they need not grasp onto possessions and wealth as though they were in limited supply.

UNIT 7—Parable of the Great Banquet / Luke 14:15-24

The Parable of the Great Banquet

¹⁵*When one of those at the table with him heard this, he said to Jesus, "Blessed is the man who will eat at the feast in the kingdom of God."*

¹⁶*Jesus replied: "A certain man was preparing a great banquet and invited many guests.* ¹⁷*At the time of the banquet he sent his servant to tell those who had been invited, 'Come, for everything is now ready.'*

¹⁸*"But they all alike began to make excuses. The first said, 'I have just bought a field, and I must go and see it. Please excuse me.'*

¹⁹*"Another said, 'I have just bought five yoke of oxen, and I'm on my way to try them out. Please excuse me.'*

²⁰*"Still another said, 'I just got married, so I can't come.'*

²¹*"The servant came back and reported this to his master. Then the owner of the house became angry and ordered his servant, 'Go out quickly into the streets and alleys of the town and bring in the poor, the crippled, the blind and the lame.'*

²²*" 'Sir,' the servant said, 'what you ordered has been done, but there is still room.'*

²³*"Then the master told his servant, 'Go out to the roads and country lanes and make them come in, so that my house will be full.* ²⁴*I tell you, not one of those men who were invited will get a taste of my banquet.' "*

READ

First Reading / First Impressions: How would you react to friends who decided at the last minute not to come to a banquet you had arranged?

❐ I'd be really hurt for a while.
❐ I'd never talk to them again.
❐ I'd write to Ann Landers.

❐ I'd find new friends.
❐ I'd change the date of the party.
❐ other:_____

Second Reading / Big Idea: In a sentence, how would you sum up the main point of this parable?

SEARCH

1. In response to Jesus having just referred to feasts and the resurrection, someone blurts out a favorite sentiment of the Jews (v. 15). Who did this person likely expect to be present at such a feast (see note on v. 15)?

2. Jesus was having dinner with a group of Pharisees when he told this parable. Who do the characters in this parable represent?

   the host:

   the three guests:

   the poor, crippled, blind and lame:

3. Wealthy people of that day received double invitations. The second invitation was on the day of the event, and let them know when the banquet was ready to be served. How would those listening to this parable feel about the three guests' excuses on the day of the banquet?

4. How might you have felt if you were one of "the poor, the crippled, the blind and the lame" (v. 21) suddenly invited to this great banquet? (Place an *"X"* on the scale below.)

| very grateful | pleased, I'm hungry | ho hum | I'd have refused, too! |

5. Why did Jesus turn what was a common Jewish sentiment (v. 15) into a disturbing parable for the Pharisees with whom he was eating? What point is Jesus making to them (see final note on v. 23)?

6. What kind of attitude did Jesus want the Pharisees to have toward his invitation to come and join in the banquet? What kind of attitude does Jesus expect of people today?

APPLY

1. What character in this passage do you identify with most in your spiritual life?
   - ❏ The first two guests—I'm interested but I just don't have time.
   - ❏ The third guest—I'm really not interested.
   - ❏ The outcast who is grateful to be invited to the banquet.
   - ❏ The outcast who needs a little coaxing to come.
   - ❏ The servant who is sent out to bring others to the party.
   - ❏ other:_____

2. What is the excuse you use most often to keep God (and his desires for you) at arm's length?

3. Is God inviting you to deepen your relationship with him? If so, what steps do you need to take to accept that invitation?

GROUP AGENDA

After the first part, read the Scripture out loud and divide into groups of 4. Then come back together for the third part.

TO BEGIN / 10–15 Min. (Choose 1 or 2)
1. Did you ever skip school or make up an excuse to get out of going?

2. What's your favorite excuse to get out of something you don't want to do now?

3. From your own experience, do you think it is easier for children of religious families to find peace with God?

TO GO DEEPER / 30 Min. (Choose 2 or 3)
1. If some in your group have done the homework, quickly go through as many of the READ and SEARCH questions as you can.

2. As Jesus told this parable, what do you think was his tone of voice, particularly toward the three guests who made excuses: Anger? Sadness? Indifference?

3. What exactly is the "great banquet"? What does it take to get in, and do you have a reservation?

4. Why do so many people say "No" to God's "banquet"? Who, in particular, can you think of? What can you say or do to help them come in?

5. CASE STUDY: At your high school reunion, you meet three old friends from your Young Life Club. All three pooh-pooh the religious experience they had in high school, and make excuses for their lack of any spiritual concern now. How do you relate to these friends?

TO CLOSE / 15–30 Min.
1. Are you happy with your group's progress on developing your mission?

2. Share at least one of your answers to the questions in APPLY.

3. Since being in this group, what has happened to your appetite for spiritual things?

4. How can the group pray for you this week?

NOTES

Summary. Chapter 14 of Luke's Gospel opens with the story of Jesus at a banquet in the home of a Pharisee. In that setting, he tells his listeners that they should not invite to their feasts and parties only those people who are in a position to repay them, but that they should invite people—like the poor and crippled—who could not be expected to do so. The repayment for these types of hosts will come when they experience the resurrection of the righteous (v. 14). The mention of the resurrection leads one of the dinner guests to express the common Jewish sentiment found in verse 15. Jesus uses this common feeling to underscore the reality of God's gracious invitation and to force his listeners to consider how they have actually responded to God's call.

14:15 _Blessed is the man._ The bliss of life with God was often pictured in terms of a feast (see Isa. 25:6; 65:13). The Jews typically assumed that the messianic banquet was reserved for righteous Jews only. To be "blessed" means to be held in God's favor. It was thought that only those Jews (who by virtue of their good works are accounted righteous) would be able to share in the feast of the Messiah.

14:16–17 _invited / sent his servant to tell._ In well-to-do circles, invitations for a formal dinner were issued well in advance, but the specific time to arrive was communicated on the day of the event when everything was ready (Est. 5:8; 6:14). The double invitation was also an indication of the importance of the guest.

14:18–20 All these people had accepted the invitation earlier. Now that the feast is actually prepared, however, they all offer excuses why they cannot come. In light of their previous acceptance (and the amount of work involved in the preparation of the banquet), Jesus' listeners would immediately see these excuses as a horrible social insult to the host. Some commentators think the excuses are modeled on the provisions for exemptions for military service given in Deuteronomy 20:5–7. When Israel faced war, men who had just bought property, or had planted a vineyard not yet harvested, or had recently married were exempt from military duty. These exceptions were practiced even during the Maccabean revolt against Rome in the second century B.C. Like Jesus' warnings elsewhere (Luke 8:14; 9:23–24,57–62; 12:15), the fact that Jesus uses these excuses demonstrates that normal business and family obligations are not valid reasons for neglecting the call of the kingdom of God. However, since the invitation is to a banquet and not a war, it is questionable whether this is the correct understanding of the excuses. It seems more likely that such excuses would have been understood as an obvious attempt to degrade the host's honor. The guests held him in such low esteem that they would not even dignify their refusal to come with believable reasons. This attitude is reflected by the religious leaders, who were too occupied with their traditions and power to respond to the invitation of Jesus to follow him (Luke 13:34).

14:18 *I have just bought a field, and I must go and see it.* Then, as now, people would not buy property first and look at it later! Besides, since banquets would be in the late afternoon, the man would have had plenty of time during the day to see it.

14:19 *I'm on my way to try them out.* Just as no one today would buy a used car without a test drive, so then a man would not buy a team of oxen unless he had already tried them out.

14:20 *married.* Marriage plans were made far in advance: the man certainly would have known of his marriage plans when he received the original invitation to the banquet. In this context, the net effect of these excuses is that they are all transparently flimsy. They in fact reflect a social snub to the host: they are in effect saying that property, oxen and marital duties are more important than their relationship to the host.

I can't come. At least the first two men politely asked to be excused. The third man simply dismisses the host and his invitation as too insignificant to warrant an apology.

14:21 *streets.* This may be the public squares where beggars would gather, hoping for handouts.

the poor, the crippled, the blind and the lame. Matthew 22:2–14 records a similar parable, but does not specify the condition of those receiving the second invitation. The kinds of people mentioned in this list were all social outcasts, unable to work and reduced to begging for survival. It was commonly assumed their suffering showed that they were being punished by God because of some serious sin they once committed. Throughout his Gospel, Luke has been especially concerned to show that those normally considered not worthy of the kingdom of God are indeed the ones who are included (Luke 1:52–53; 4:18–19; 6:20–22; 7:22). The irony is highlighted when it is remembered that people with such defects were typically thought of as ritually impure, unable to participate in temple worship, and ineligible for taking part in the coming final battle (which would usher in the messianic kingdom for Israel). Jesus shatters these ideas. The kingdom is precisely for these types of people. In contrast, those who were always thought to be "pure" will be excluded. Donahue points out how Jesus shifts attention away from the common apocalyptic expectation of the messianic banquet (as a future, climactic event reserved for the ritually and morally pure) to emphasize how disciples ought to relate to their Lord and to others in the here and now. God's kingdom has come now, and the way disciples treat those who are ordinarily thought to be outcasts (even in religious circles) is a mark of how fully the disciples have caught on to the presence of the King in their midst.

14:23 Since the banquet cannot be filled with only the poor from the city, the servant is sent out to the country to bring in others. Matthew's version of the parable lacks this third invitation to those outside the city. Given Luke's concern for the inclusion of Gentiles in the kingdom of God, he may have included this as a way of foreshadowing the extension of the kingdom of God to include Gentiles (Acts 1:8).

make them come in. This phrase has been unfortunately used in the past to justify forced baptisms and other practices that used political, social or physical pressure to get people to become members of the church. Such practices run counter to the whole spirit of Jesus. The persuasion in view here is simply meant to convince these incredulous outcasts that they really are welcomed to the banquet. Middle East etiquette requires people of a low social rank to refuse invitations from those of a higher social status. The understanding is that such invitations are polite gestures but are not meant to be accepted.

not one ... will get a taste. It was common for the host of a banquet to send portions of food to those unable to attend. This will not be done in this case because the host will see that the poor eat all of it. None will be left to send to the others. The immediate point of the parable is to warn the religiously privileged Jewish leaders (many of whom were at this banquet—Luke 14:3). Their refusal to come to the banquet (which Jesus announced) was rooted in arrogance, and thus was an insult to God. Others will come, but those who refuse the invitation will be excluded (Luke 13:22–30). Hendriksen states, "the one central lesson of the parable is: Accept God's gracious invitation. Do it now!"

UNIT 8—The Builder and the King / Luke 14:25-35

The Cost of Being a Disciple

²⁵Large crowds were traveling with Jesus, and turning to them he said: ²⁶"If anyone comes to me and does not hate his father and mother, his wife and children, his brothers and sisters—yes, even his own life—he cannot be my disciple. ²⁷And anyone who does not carry his cross and follow me cannot be my disciple.

²⁸"Suppose one of you wants to build a tower. Will he not first sit down and estimate the cost to see if he has enough money to complete it? ²⁹For if he lays the foundation and is not able to finish it, everyone who sees it will ridicule him, ³⁰saying, 'This fellow began to build and was not able to finish.'

³¹"Or suppose a king is about to go to war against another king. Will he not first sit down and consider whether he is able with ten thousand men to oppose the one coming against him with twenty thousand? ³²If he is not able, he will send a delegation while the other is still a long way off and will ask for terms of peace. ³³In the same way, any of you who does not give up everything he has cannot be my disciple.

³⁴"Salt is good, but if it loses its saltiness, how can it be made salty again? ³⁵It is fit neither for the soil nor for the manure pile; it is thrown out.

"He who has ears to hear, let him hear."

READ

First Reading / First Impressions: Which statement best reflects your initial reaction to this passage?

❑ This makes me stop and take notice—it's pretty sobering talk.

❑ This excites me—I love a real challenge.

❑ This scares me—I don't think I've thought a lot about what is involved in following Jesus.

❑ This confuses me—it sounds so extreme.

Second Reading / Big Idea: What is Jesus' point with these three illustrations (tower, king, salt)?

SEARCH

1. Given Jesus' enormous popularity (v. 25), why might he have said what he did in verses 26–27?

2. What does Jesus mean when he says we must "hate" our families (v. 26; see note)?

3. What did the idea of a person "carrying his cross" (v. 27; see note) mean to Jesus' listeners and Luke's readers? What does it mean to us today?

4. According to common wisdom, what do you do prior to beginning to build a structure (v. 28)? What is the result if you don't do this?

FOUNDATION

5. According to common wisdom, what would a king do prior to going to war with another king (vv. 31–32)? What is the result if a king does not do this?

DESERT

6. What is Jesus saying we need to do prior to deciding to be a disciple of his (see note on v. 33)? What might be the result if we fail to do this?

BUILDING ON FOUNDATION
Defeat

7. What does the salt analogy (vv. 34–35) emphasize about discipleship?

APPLY

1. Since discipleship costs so much, what keeps you going? Why not choose an easier way?

2. Write a personal prayer to God based on this passage. Include any commitments, requests for help, or questions that arise from your reflections (e.g., Dear God, I want to commit to you my ... . I need help in my relationship with ... . Does this passage mean I need to give up my ... ?).

GROUP AGENDA

After the first part, read the Scripture out loud and divide into groups of 4. Then come back together for the third part.

TO BEGIN / 10–15 Min. (Choose 1 or 2)
1. What's something you saved for or planned for a long time: A car? House? Vacation?

2. In your family, who decides the budget and any cuts in the budget?

3. How heavily do you use table salt? How easily could you tolerate a salt-free diet?

TO GO DEEPER / 30 Min. (Choose 2 or 3)
1. Based on the homework questions and the study notes, what does this passage in general and these three parables in particular tell us about following Jesus?

2. What do you think caused Jesus to suddenly get tough in his teaching? If we did the same today, what would happen to the "crowds" at church?

3. People in Jesus' day wrongly thought God's kingdom would mean prosperity, power and freedom from Rome. What misguided ideas do people have today about the results of being a Christian?

4. When you gave your life to Christ, how much did you understand about what you were getting into?

5. Dietrich Bonhoeffer, a leader of the Nazi resistance in Hitler's Germany, said, "Grace is free, but it is not cheap." How true have you found that to be in your experience?

6. CASE STUDY: "When I married you, I didn't expect to be marrying some religious fanatic." This is the way Tom explained it when he left his wife for another woman. Now, she struggles to raise the three kids—with Tom doing everything he can to undermine their faith. If she were in your group, what could the group do?

TO CLOSE / 15–30 Min.
1. Share your answer to at least one question in APPLY.

2. In comparison to what following Christ has cost multitudes of suffering Christians, how much has following Christ cost you? How willing are you to "give up everything" you have for Christ?

3. How can the group pray for you?

NOTES

Summary. While the previous scene used the context of a private dinner party to stress the fact that the invitation to God's kingdom is extended to all types of people (Luke 14:1–24), this scene involves a huge crowd flocking after Jesus. In this context, Jesus lays stress on the serious implications involved in becoming one of his disciples. His intent is not to discourage people from following him, but to give them a clearheaded picture of what discipleship really means. Since the crowds expected the Messiah to bring about a golden age of victory for the Jews (which would insure their prosperity and freedom), it was especially important that they realize the true nature of what discipleship involved. Before the kingdom would fully come, Jesus had to face the Cross. The fact that the Messiah would suffer (and that his people would as well) was not a reality they had comprehended.

14:25 *Large crowds were traveling with Jesus.* Jesus is heading toward Jerusalem for Passover (Luke 9:51). This crowd probably consisted of other pilgrims on the way to the feast as well. The expectations would have been high that Jesus, if he was indeed the Messiah, would begin the establishment of his kingdom at this feast (since it was the celebration of Israel's deliverance from Egypt centuries before). Now the crowd would be expecting him to lead them in deliverance from Rome.

14:26 In contrast to the expectant, exuberant nature of the crowds, Jesus introduces a solemn challenge. While the invitation to the kingdom is extended to all, only those who make Jesus their primary loyalty will participate in it. One's loyalty to Jesus and the kingdom must take precedence over all other commitments, including those that people normally take for granted as primary responsibilities.

comes to me. This is to take on the role of a disciple, one committed to the teachings of a master.

hate. Jesus often used dramatic, overstated examples to arrest people's attention and make his point (see Matt. 5:29–30). His use of the word "hate" here is a hyperbolic way of saying that our love and loyalty to Jesus must exceed what we naturally have toward our family. The disciple is to view even normal and ordinarily proper concerns, ambitions and interests as secondary in importance to the kingdom of God. "Jesus calls not for an unloving attitude, but for a willingness to put him first in the concrete situation where the calls of Jesus and of family conflict" (France). This idea is stated more positively in

Matthew 10:37–38 which reads, "Anyone who loves his father or mother more than me is not worthy of me; anyone who loves his son or daughter more than me is not worthy of me; and anyone who does not take his cross and follow me is not worthy of me."

even his own life. Even the instinctive drive for self-preservation must give way to obedience to the call of Jesus. While this seems like a harsh demand, Jesus himself practiced it as he gave his life in order to bring life to others.

14:27 carry his cross. This symbolized the grisly method of Roman execution. While it had a very literal application for some disciples, it is meant as a metaphor emphasizing the need for all of Jesus' disciples to put to death their own desires and interests for the sake of loyalty to Jesus. This statement echoes the one in Luke 9:23, where Luke inserts the word "daily," indicating that following Jesus is a day-by-day decision in light of the new pressures and conflicts one continually faces.

14:28–33 Jesus uses three parables to communicate the need for serious consideration of what it means to be his disciple.

14:28–30 The first parable relates to the daily experience of Jesus' audience. The tower in view might be a vineyard tower used as a lookout to watch for thieves, a storage shed, or some other type of farm building. It would be humiliating to have to stop construction because of planning so poorly that money ran out after only the foundation was completed. In the same way, one must consider the implications of following Jesus. To do so is a commitment of one's entire life and resources. Just as it would be foolish to begin building a tower before contemplating the costs involved, so Jesus is discouraging people from following him based upon wrong assumptions and ideas of what his kingdom involves.

14:31–32 The second parable reinforces the point of the first. Only a foolish king would attempt to wage a war before considering whether there is realistic hope for success. If the enemy has a far superior force, it would be far better to make a peaceful settlement before hostilities begin than to plunge into destruction. Likewise, a would-be disciple had better first consider what is involved in the course he or she is undertaking. Jesus is not interested in having people following him who are misguided by false expectations.

14:33 any of you who does not give up everything he has. The point of both parables is here: "... discipleship means saying a final 'good-bye' to one's possessions (and all other loyalties, ambitions, etc.). Just as one should not attempt a venture without having sufficient resources to complete it, but will need to put everything into it in order to be successful, so the disciple must be continually ready ... to give up all that he has got in order to follow Jesus" (Marshall).

14:34 The final parable builds on the point of the earlier two as it looks at the fate of those who make only a partial attempt to follow Jesus and the way of the kingdom.

Salt is good. Good salt was used to preserve and flavor food. It was also used in small amounts as a way of fertilizing soil and manure to be more productive for the bearing of crops (as is reflected in verse 35).

if it loses its saltiness. True salt, of course, never loses its saltiness. However, Jesus is commenting on what was a common observation of the time for people who lived around the Dead Sea. The evaporation of water from the Dead Sea resulted in white crystals. Some of these crystals were true salt, but others, although they physically looked like salt, were gypsum (which was either bitter or stale). Thus, it appeared that some "salt" was good and other "salt" had apparently somehow lost its valuable properties. While people of the time did not know the chemical realities involved, they did know that there was no way such useless "salt" could ever be restored.

14:35 it is thrown out. While the useless crystals looked the same as real salt, they had no function other than to serve as road dust. Failure to persevere with Jesus is to be like these crystals which, while they have the appearance of being real, are worthless.

He who has ears to hear, let him hear. This is a common phrase Jesus used in other contexts as well (see Luke 8:8; Mark 4:9,23). Jesus urges his hearers to ponder his parables. Part of the power of a parable lies in the fact that a person must reflect on it in order to understand it. The question is: What insight do you need to grasp about your spiritual life from these simple stories?

UNIT 9—The Parable of the Tenants / Mark 12:1–12

The Parable of the Tenants

12 He then began to speak to them in parables: "A man planted a vineyard. He put a wall around it, dug a pit for the winepress and built a watchtower. Then he rented the vineyard to some farmers and went away on a journey. ²At harvest time he sent a servant to the tenants to collect from them some of the fruit of the vineyard. ³But they seized him, beat him and sent him away empty-handed. ⁴Then he sent another servant to them; they struck this man on the head and treated him shamefully. ⁵He sent still another, and that one they killed. He sent many others; some of them they beat, others they killed.

⁶"He had one left to send, a son, whom he loved. He sent him last of all, saying, 'They will respect my son.'

⁷"But the tenants said to one another, 'This is the heir. Come, let's kill him, and the inheritance will be ours.' ⁸So they took him and killed him, and threw him out of the vineyard.

⁹"What then will the owner of the vineyard do? He will come and kill those tenants and give the vineyard to others. ¹⁰Haven't you read this scripture:

" 'The stone the builders rejected
   has become the capstone;
¹¹the Lord has done this, and it is
   marvelous in our eyes'?"

¹²Then they looked for a way to arrest him because they knew he had spoken the parable against them. But they were afraid of the crowd; so they left him and went away.

READ

First Reading / First Impressions: What emotions do you sense as this parable is told?

☒ anger   ☐ guilt   ☐ sadness

☐ shock   ☐ repulsion   ☐ other:_____

Second Reading / Big Idea: What phrase or slogan might you use to sum up the point of this parable?

Repulsion

SEARCH

1. Skim Mark 11:12–33. What facts about the background in that section are important in understanding the setting of this parable (see Summary in notes)?

*The Lord gave life to man; it
Was able to give life to priest*

2. Before proceeding, read Isaiah 5:1–7, a poem that provides the image Jesus uses here. Unlike most parables of Jesus, this parable is an allegory (in which each detail represents something). Given that, what is represented by each of the following?

the vineyard:

the owner:

the tenant-farmers:

the owner's servants:

the owner's son:

the new tenants:

3. How does the Scripture Jesus quotes (vv. 10–11) relate to the parable? Who is the rejected stone and who are the builders?

4. How did the religious leaders feel about this parable? Why did they react the way they did (see note on v. 6)?

5. How do you suppose Mark's first readers, the early church, would have reacted to this event from Jesus' life? How might they feel about the Jewish religious establishment, Jesus' prophecy of his own death, and even the beginning of their own church?

APPLY

1. How do you welcome Jesus in your life on a daily basis?

2. What actions of yours might make Jesus feel unwelcome in your life?

3. The tendency most groups, ministries and churches have as they age is to become more institutionalized—preserving the organizational traditions and being less open to new developments. If this is true, how would the teachings of this parable serve as a warning to the group, ministry or church in which you participate?

GROUP AGENDA

After the first part, read the Scripture out loud and divide into groups of 4. Then come back together for the third part.

TO BEGIN / 10–15 Min. (Choose 1 or 2)
1. What was your first landlord (or dorm supervisor, apartment manager, etc.) like?

2. When you are away, who do you have take care of your home, yard, pet, etc.? Do you worry while you're gone?

3. How do you handle rejection?

TO GO DEEPER / 30 Min. (Choose 2 or 3)
1. If you have completed the homework, what stands out to you from the READ and SEARCH questions or the study notes?

2. Why did Jesus challenge the Jewish religious leaders so strongly?

3. If Jesus were nominated to fill a vacancy on the Supreme Court, what do you think the reaction would be in the Senate confirmation hearings? Would he get confirmed?

4. What is the message in this parable for our country? For religious institutions of today? For you personally?

5. CASE STUDY: Last week, Donna's 20-year-old daughter moved in with her boyfriend. Donna was shocked. "How could she do this to us," Donna asks you, "after all we have sacrificed for her?" What do you say?

TO CLOSE / 15–30 Min.
1. Has your group assigned three people as a leadership core to start a new small group?

2. Share your answer to at least one of the questions in APPLY.

3. What specific "vineyards" has God entrusted to you? How is the harvest coming?

4. How can the group support you in prayer?

NOTES

Summary. This parable (also found in Matt. 21:33–46 and Luke 20:9–19) immediately follows the controversy Jesus stirred up by his radical action of driving out the money changers in the temple (Mark 11:12–19). The religious authorities who challenged his right to do such a thing were silenced by his artful response, which put the religious leaders in the politically impossible position of either denouncing John the Baptist as a false prophet, or explaining why they failed to heed his word (Mark 11:27–33). While this dilemma led them to back off from their confrontation with Jesus, he refused to simply leave them in their confusion. Instead, Jesus kept up the pressure by speaking this parable which, while it was addressed to the crowd at large, was clearly directed at the leaders. In no uncertain terms, Jesus was asserting that the leaders of Israel (who have turned against both him and John the Baptist) have rejected God's messengers and so face the prospect of divine judgment.

12:1 *parables.* Typically, a parable has a single point. In such parables, details simply add to the setting of the story. This parable is more of an allegory (in that a number of details have meaning).

A man planted a vineyard ... dug a pit ... built a watchtower. For the religious leaders, Jesus' use of these phrases would surely call to mind the well-known imagery found in a poem originally delivered by the prophet Isaiah centuries before (Isa. 5:1–7). In Isaiah's song, the symbol of the vineyard was used to describe Israel. Although planted and cultivated by God, Israel was compared to a vineyard that produced only bad fruit. As a result, the landowner destroyed it. With this similarity established in Isaiah's poem, Jesus goes on to make a significant difference: Isaiah identified the unresponsive vineyard as the nation of Israel as a whole, whereas Jesus focuses attention on the fact that Israel's leaders are like evil tenants who refused to acknowledge God's authority over them.

vineyard. Since grapes were one of the major crops in Israel, a vineyard would be something known to everyone. Grapes were eaten fresh, made into raisins, boiled into a syrup, or made into wine.

a wall. The wall would be to keep out animals and thieves.

a pit. The pit was a place in which the grapes were crushed to make wine.

a watchtower. This was a structure in the midst of

the vineyard from which the farmer could keep a lookout for robbers. During the harvest, the farmer would even spend the night in the watchtower. The wall, pit, and tower all emphasize that the farmer intended that this vineyard be productive, since he made such an investment of money and labor in it.

went away. Jesus changes the Isaiah poem here in order to put the spotlight on the religious authorities (who were the leaders of Israel). In Isaiah, God is the farmer who waits for the fruit which never appears; in this parable, God is the landlord who leaves his vineyard in the care of others who are responsible to him. It produces fruit, but the tenants refuse to give him his share of the produce. Absentee landlords were common in the first century, especially in Galilee. Such a landlord would get tenant-farmers to work his large estate, requiring them to give him a portion of their harvest in payment for use of the land. The tenant-farmers frequently resented the landlord.

12:2 servant. The landowner's servant came in the name of the landowner and should have been given the proceeds due to the landowner. In terms of this parable, the servants represent the Old Testament prophets. In the Old Testament, prophets were frequently referred to in this way (see Jer. 7:25–26; Zech. 1:6). The fate of the servants in this parable (vv. 2–5) was the same for many of God's prophets. Elijah was scorned by King Ahab. Tradition holds that Isaiah was executed by being sawn in two. Jeremiah faced many struggles, including being cast into a cistern to starve, and being taken as a prisoner to Egypt (where, tradition teaches, he was killed). John the Baptist, believed by the crowds here in this scene to be a prophet, was beheaded by King Herod with no word of protest from the religious leaders.

12:3–5 The tenants refused to acknowledge the landowner's rights and badly abused those he sent as his representatives.

12:6 a son, whom he loved. Neither the crowd nor the religious leaders would have known the identity of the son in this story. The context of the controversy (in which the leaders were rejecting the authority of Jesus) would suggest to the leaders that Jesus was referring to himself, yet he does not explicitly say so. This would create another level of controversy among the leaders. Not only would they be upset at Jesus for identifying them as the evil tenants, but they would also be angered over this

implicit claim to be the beloved son of God. While the leaders and the crowd may be confused over who the son represents, Mark's readers know that this is clearly a reference to Jesus.

They will respect my son. While the servants had been badly abused, the landowner assumed the tenants would not dare treat his own son with such contempt.

12:7 inheritance. The arrival of the son was mistakenly understood by the servants as a sign that the landowner must have died. Assuming that the son had come to claim his inheritance, they decided to take decisive action. By law, a piece of ownerless property could be kept by those who first occupied and cultivated it. Since the tenants assumed the land would be ownerless if the son was dead, they plotted to kill him in order to lay claim to the land for themselves.

12:8 killed him, and threw him out of the vineyard. Not only did the tenants fail to respect the son, but they even refused to give him a proper burial. This would have been considered a monstrous indignity to the listeners. Mark's readers, of course, would see the parallels with what happened with Jesus who was crucified, and whose body the religious leaders would have been content to leave hanging on the cross, were it not for the intervention of Joseph of Arimathea (Mark 15:43).

12:9 The final rejection moves the landowner to take action personally. His sudden, unexpected appearance would shatter the illusion that the tenants now owned the land. The owner could enlist the aid of the government to execute judgment upon the tenants.

give the vineyard to others. The implication in the parable is that God will raise up new leaders to care for his people. In the context in which Mark was written (to Christians in Rome), this was probably understood as an explanation as to why the leadership in the church was becoming filled by more and more Gentiles. By the second century the church consisted almost completely of Gentiles.

12:10 The stone the builders rejected has become the capstone. This quote is from Psalm 118:22. In that context, it refers to how God established David as king even when his enemies attempted to defeat him. In the parable, the stone is Jesus (the Messiah) whom the builders (the leaders) fail to recognize.

UNIT 10—The Parable of the Talents / Matt. 25:14-30

The Parable of the Talents

[14]*"Again, it will be like a man going on a journey, who called his servants and entrusted his property to them.* [15]*To one he gave five talents of money, to another two talents, and to another one talent, each according to his ability. Then he went on his journey.* [16]*The man who had received the five talents went at once and put his money to work and gained five more.* [17]*So also, the one with the two talents gained two more.* [18]*But the man who had received the one talent went off, dug a hole in the ground and hid his master's money.*

[19]*"After a long time the master of those servants returned and settled accounts with them.* [20]*The man who had received the five talents brought the other five. 'Master,' he said, 'you entrusted me with five talents. See, I have gained five more.'*

[21]*"His master replied, 'Well done, good and faithful servant! You have been faithful with a few things; I will put you in charge of many things. Come and share your master's happiness!'*

[22]*The man with the two talents also came. 'Master,' he said. 'you entrusted me with two talents; see, I have gained two more.'*

[23]*"His master replied, 'Well done, good and faithful servant! You have been faithful with a few things; I will put you in charge of many things. Come and share your master's happiness!"*

[24]*"Then the man who had received the one talent came. 'Master,' he said, 'I knew that you are a hard man, harvesting where you have not sown and gathering where you have not scattered seed.* [25]*So I was afraid and went out and hid your talent in the ground. See, here is what belongs to you.'*

[26]*"His master replied, 'You wicked, lazy servant! So you knew that I harvest where I have not sown and gather where I have not scattered seed?* [27]*Well then, you should have put my money on deposit with the bankers, so that when I returned I would have received it back with interest.*

[28]*" 'Take the talent from him and give it to the one who has the ten talents.* [29]*For everyone who has will be given more, and he will have an abundance. Whoever does not have, even what he has will be taken from him.* [30]*And throw that worthless servant outside, into the darkness, where there will be weeping and gnashing of teeth.' "*

READ

First Reading / First Impressions: What would the *Wall Street Journal* call the way the master in the parable treated his servants?

❑ shrewd   ❑ businesslike   ❑ fair   ❑ unfair

Second Reading / Big Idea: What do you see as the one or two key ideas here?

SEARCH

1. What were the master's expectations of his servants while he was away? What are Jesus' expectations of his followers while they await his return?

Master's expectations	Jesus' expectations

2. What kind of reward do the faithful servants receive from the master (see notes on v. 21)?

3. Why do you think the servant with one talent did nothing with it other than hide it (see notes)?

4. What is the future for those who are unfaithful while Jesus is gone?

5. What is the point of this parable?

APPLY

1. The parable raises the question of whether the master is generous and gracious (vv. 21,23) or harsh and demanding (v. 24). In your experience, how has your view of God affected the way you take risks with your abilities and resources and invest them for God's kingdom?

> When I am sure he is the good and gracious Master, I tend to …
>
> When I think he is harsh or when I am unsure if he really is the Master, I tend to …

2. What "talents" has God entrusted into your keeping for investment in his kingdom? How are you using these talents and working at developing them more?

3. What motivates you to use your time, resources and abilities for God's kingdom?
   - ❏ fear of the Master
   - ❏ people's appreciation
   - ❏ God's approval
   - ❏ a chance for greater responsibility
   - ❏ fellowship with the Master
   - ❏ earthly rewards
   - ❏ rewards in the next life
   - ❏ doing the best I can with the abilities God has given me

GROUP AGENDA

After the first part, read the Scripture out loud and divide into groups of 4. Then come back together for the third part.

TO BEGIN / 10–15 Min. (Choose 1 or 2)

1. Who in your family is likely to win the Monopoly game? What is his or her strategy?

2. What's the best financial investment or decision you ever made? What's the worst?

3. If this group put on a talent show, what would you do?

TO GO DEEPER / 30 Min. (Choose 2 or 3)

1. If you have done the homework, what stands out to you from the READ or SEARCH sections? Specifically, what do you see as the message of this parable?

2. To double your money you have to take chances and work hard. Do you think this also applies to your spiritual life?

3. When it comes to the work of the kingdom, are you as conscientious as you are about your own affairs or work?

4. CASE STUDY: George is an executive of a small business. He systematically plans for 10% growth in his business every year, and he has exceeded this growth rate every year for the past 10 years. He also sits on the board of his church which has remained stagnant for the last 10 years. If this were a business, what would happen to the executive board?

TO CLOSE / 15–30 Min.

1. Share your answers to at least one of the questions in APPLY.

2. Go around the group and have each person listen silently while others affirm the "talents" God has given that person to invest in the kingdom.

3. In light of the combined talents and assets of the people in your group, what does this affirmation time say about the challenge for your group to "give birth" to a new small group?

4. How can the group help you in prayer this week?

NOTES

Summary. This parable is a different version of the one in Luke 19:11–27. While sharing a common story, the authors apply it in different ways. The major emphasis of the parable in Luke is to prepare the disciples for the delay in the coming of God's kingdom, and to warn the enemies of Jesus regarding their fate when Christ's kingdom comes. Matthew uses the parable as the third of four stories to: (1) encourage the disciples to continue in active service for the kingdom, even while its appearance is delayed, and (2) warn the disciples not to be negligent of their responsibilities in light of the judgment which, though delayed, is sure to come (Matt. 24:42–44). By means of the parable, Jesus underscores three points to the disciples: (1) His kingdom as they imagine it will not be established at this time; (2) Discipleship means faithful service to God while awaiting Christ's return; and (3) Judgment awaits those who fail to invest themselves in the work of the kingdom.

25:14 *a man ... called his servants and entrusted his property to them.* Wealthy people who had to travel on business would entrust their resources to capable servants who would act as managers of the estate. Their responsibility was to look after their master's interests in his absence, investing his resources in a way that would earn more money for him.

25:15 *five talents.* A talent was originally a unit of weight, but was also used as the name for the highest denomination of coinage. While exact modern parallels are impossible to make, it has been noted that in the time of Jesus it would take a laborer almost 20 years to earn the equivalent of one talent! Our use of "talent" as an ability comes from this parable.

each according to his ability. The master took into account the level of responsibility he believed each servant could handle. Each would be evaluated only in terms of what had been entrusted to him.

25:16–18 Like today, investing money always carried with it the risk that one might lose it. Yet two of the servants are reported as having had very good returns on their investments. The third servant, however, failed to do anything constructive with the money he was given to manage.

25:16 *gained five more.* High interest rates in that time could make a thousand percent return possible (though undoubtedly difficult).

25:18 *dug a hole in the ground and hid his master's money.* In the absence of safe deposit boxes, this was not an uncommon way of protecting one's money from being stolen. This would have been considered a safe way to protect money, but obviously its investment possibilities are nil!

25:19 *After a long time.* The indefinite time reference is to prepare the disciples for the realization that the final coming of the kingdom is still far off. They should not be surprised at its delay.

settled accounts. This was the time of reckoning, when the master would evaluate how the various servants had done in fulfilling their responsibility.

25:21 *Well done, good and faithful servant.* The servant is rewarded, not with a life of ease, but with greater administrative responsibility in the master's household (based on the master's trust and confidence in him). While five talents is by no means something small, the point is that they are "a few things" in comparison with the responsibility he will now be entrusted to handle.

Come and share your master's happiness! The servant is not only given more responsibility, but now is invited to enjoy camaraderie with the master. The relationship has shifted from simply a master/servant arrangement to one of friendship and mutual respect.

25:24–25 In contrast to the other two, this servant had simply hidden the money away where it did no good. The servant's reasoning for doing so was based on his fear of failing to live up to the master's high expectations. He assumed it would be better to safely return the money rather than risk having to make up any loss he may have incurred by making a bad investment.

25:24 *a hard man.* Literally, this is "exacting." The description of the master is uncomplimentary; it pictures him as ruthless, harvesting for himself the fruits for which other people have worked. While the inclinations of the listeners (who were poor) might naturally lead them to favor the servant over a "hard" rich man, nothing in the story so far indicates that the servant's characterization of the master was correct. He was generous in his original entrustment of his property to the servants. He was generous to the first and second servants upon his return. It would raise the question in the listeners' minds as to whether the servant was correct or just irresponsible in light of such a generous master's trust.

25:25 *So I was afraid.* The servant implies that his lack of having anything to show for having been entrusted with the talent is really the fault of the master: He expects too much; he is too frightening.

25:26–27 The servant stands condemned by his own words. Whether or not his assessment of the master was correct, if he felt that the master was like this he should have at least tried to make some safe investments so that there would be at least a little bit of profit to show.

25:26 *You wicked, lazy servant.* The master turns the tables on the servant. It was not out of fear of him that the servant acted as he did; it was because he did not have the master's interests at heart. His action did not betray a wise fear of the master's authority, but simply neglect of his responsibility. If the servant was so certain of the master's character, he would have been sure to have done something so that he would not have to face the master with nothing to show for the master's trust in him.

25:28–30 Judgment is pronounced upon this servant. The faithless servant loses the capital he had been given, while it is added to the interest of the most faithful servant. By doing so, the master shows that the faithless servant's characterization of him as hard and miserly is false. The point of this part of the parable is to warn the disciples to apply themselves to the task of serving Jesus with all diligence. "There is no such thing as standing still in the Christian life" (Barclay). God expects those to whom he has entrusted various gifts to be faithful and diligent in their use of them for his purposes.

25:29 *everyone who has ... Whoever does not have.* The judgment is justified by use of a common saying found in other contexts as well (Matt. 13:12; Mark 4:25; Luke 8:18). The saying illustrates a spiritual principle about discipleship that has many implications. In brief, those who hear and practice the word from God that they have been given are those who will be able to understand and receive more from God. Those who neglect what they have already heard will not be given any more.

25:30 *throw that worthless servant outside, into the darkness, where there will be weeping and gnashing of teeth.* This is a graphic, stock phrase often used to express the severity of God's judgment (see Matt. 8:12; 13:42,50; 22:13; 24:5; Luke 13:28).

UNIT 11—The Workers in the Vineyard / Matt. 20:1-16

The Parable of the Workers in the Vineyard

20 "For the kingdom of heaven is like a landowner who went out early in the morning to hire men to work in his vineyard. ²He agreed to pay them a denarius for the day and sent them into his vineyard.

³"About the third hour he went out and saw others standing in the marketplace doing nothing. ⁴He told them, 'You also go and work in my vineyard, and I will pay you whatever is right.' ⁵So they went.

"He went out again about the sixth hour and the ninth hour and did the same thing. ⁶About the eleventh hour he went out and found still others standing around. He asked them, 'Why have you been standing here all day long doing nothing?'

⁷" 'Because no one has hired us,' they answered.

"He said to them, 'You also go and work in my vineyard.'

⁸"When evening came, the owner of the vineyard said to his foreman, 'Call the workers and pay them their wages, beginning with the last ones hired and going on to the first.'

⁹"The workers who were hired about the eleventh hour came and each received a denarius. ¹⁰So when those came who were hired first, they expected to receive more. But each one of them also received a denarius. ¹¹When they received it, they began to grumble against the landowner. ¹²'These men who were hired last worked only one hour,' they said, 'and you have made them equal to us who have borne the burden of the work and the heat of the day.'

¹³"But he answered one of them, 'Friend, I am not being unfair to you. Didn't you agree to work for a denarius? ¹⁴Take your pay and go. I want to give the man who was hired last the same as I gave you. ¹⁵Don't I have the right to do what I want with my own money? Or are you envious because I am generous?'

¹⁶"So the last will be first, and the first will be last."

READ

First Reading / First Impressions: If you worked for a temporary service agency, how would you like to work for an employer like this?

Second Reading / Big Idea: How would you retitle this parable to catch a bit more of its meaning?

SEARCH

1. Landowners typically hired day-laborers to help at certain times when the demands of the crop exceeded the ability of their regular servants. What wage agreement did the landowner make with the original people he hired at 6 a.m. (see notes on v. 2)?

2. What wage agreement did the landowner have with the laborers he hired at 9 a.m., noon, 3 p.m., and 5 p.m. (see note on v. 4)?

3. When pay time came at 6 p.m., how would you have felt if you were in the 5 p.m. shift (vv. 8–9)?

4. How would you have felt if you were in the 6 a.m. shift (vv. 11–12)?

5. In your own words, what is the owner's response to the grumbling men (vv. 13–15)?

6. This parable is meant to say something about the kingdom of heaven (v. 1). What insights about the kingdom does this parable give regarding:

God's character?

the real basis of reward?

the status of people in the kingdom?

APPLY

1. One group sees the landowner as unfair, while the others see him as generous. When have you struggled between these two different views of God? Why?

2. Suppose a friend read this parable and said to you, "Aha! You work so hard now at trying to live for God, but you won't get anything more out of it than I will when I decide to convert when I'm 80. So I'll get the best of both worlds!" How would you respond?

3. Do you ever wish you had waited to "go to work" in God's "vineyard," or feel jealous of others who waited until the "eleventh hour"?

GROUP AGENDA

After the first part, read the Scripture out loud and divide into groups of 4. Then come back together for the third part.

TO BEGIN / 10–15 Min. (Choose 1 or 2)
1. What was your first paying job, and how much did you get paid?

2. Have you ever worked as a temporary where you were hired by the day?

3. What is most unfair about your workplace?

TO GO DEEPER / 30 Min. (Choose 2 or 3)
1. How does your sense of fairness react when you read this parable?

2. Based on the homework assignment, what is the big lesson you learned here? How does this parable add to your understanding of the Gospel, God's grace, and your own "merit"?

3. If you have lived a moral life, how much does it bother you to think that those who haven't can receive the same benefits of the kingdom?

4. CASE STUDY: Steve is a baby boomer: age 48, a good job, three kids, two cars, a nice home, and a pension when he retires. One of his kids is a baby buster: age 24, no house, no car, no job, and no future. College-trained for a job that does not exist, he sits around the house, waiting for job offers that never come. "I'm not going to work for less than I'm worth, or at a job below my dignity." What is the word of grace for this baby buster, and for his baby boomer father?

TO CLOSE / 15–30 Min.
1. How did your group answer the three "Brainstorming" questions on page M19 in the center section?

2. Share your answer to at least one of the questions in APPLY.

3. Regarding your energy level and attitude toward life, what "time" is it for you right now: 6 a.m.— raring to go? 9 a.m.—feeling productive? Noon—ready for a break? 3 p.m.—running out of gas? 5 p.m.—Help, I *am* out of gas? 6 p.m.— feeling good about what I've accomplished?

4. How can the group support you in prayer?

54

NOTES

Summary. This parable follows Jesus' response to the disciples' concern about who will be able to enter God's kingdom (Matt. 19:25). Jesus assured them that those who follow him will receive far more than they ever gave up in order to become disciples. He then adds, "But many who are first will be last, and many who are last will be first" (Matt. 19:30), a phrase echoed at the end of this parable (v. 16— see also Luke 13:30). The point of the saying is to relieve the disciples of any notion that the length of time a person knows Jesus has any bearing on one's ultimate relationship with him. The nature of one's relationship with Jesus is a matter of God's grace, not a matter of how one has ranked in time or how much religious merit one has tried to accumulate. This would have been an issue for the church in Matthew's day in a couple of ways: (1) They may have wondered if their discipleship was somehow second-rate (since they had not actually been with Jesus personally); and (2) They may have wondered if the Gentiles (who were rapidly becoming the majority in the Christian community) really were entitled to the same status in God's kingdom as they (the original Jewish believers) were. The parable's stress is on the fact that a person's status in the kingdom is a matter of God's grace and not a reward for the longevity of one's work for God.

20:1 *to hire men to work in his vineyard.* Landowners had full-time servants who took care of the daily needs of the estate, but at certain times (such as at planting, pruning or harvest) they would hire day laborers to help with work that the regular servants could not do on their own. At these times, men would gather in the village and hope that they might be hired.

vineyard. Since the Old Testament often used a vineyard as a metaphor for Israel (Isa. 5:1–7; Jer. 12:10), it may be that the vineyard here is meant to suggest Israel. The workers are then those who are called to care for (and tend to) Israel.

20:2 *He agreed to pay them.* The implication is that this was a negotiated arrangement. Bargaining back and forth was a common way for people in the Middle East to do business (as offers and counteroffers would be made). Since the landowner needed workers for that day, the laborers were in a position to negotiate a bit.

a denarius. This was a subsistence wage. Apparently, this was considered a fair wage for a day's work.

20:3 *the third hour.* This is 9 a.m.

doing nothing. By this time in the morning, if no one had hired the workers it was unlikely that they would get work that day.

the marketplace. This was the gathering place for a village. It would be a natural place for people looking for work to go in hopes of meeting someone who would be able to hire them.

20:4 *I will pay you whatever is right.* Since these workers had no reasonable prospects for work that day, they were not in much of a position to bargain. Whatever the landowner paid them would be better than nothing. There is no negotiation about the wage; just the promise that the landowner will not exploit them. Since those hired first agreed to a denarius, the expectation is set up among the listeners of the parable that these men would receive some fraction of that.

20:5 *the sixth hour.* This is noontime.

the ninth hour. This is 3 p.m. For the landowner to have to keep going to the marketplace to find workers indicates that the job (probably gathering a harvest) was more demanding than expected. It would be important to gather in a harvest as quickly as possible so it would not be spoiled by rain or rot.

20:6–7 This scene "recalls, implies and summarizes the householder's previous dealings with 'the others' " (Scott).

20:6 *the eleventh hour.* This is 5 p.m. The listeners would have been surprised that the landowner was still hiring people this late in the day.

20:8–12 The landowner settles accounts with his workers. While the landowner's last-minute hiring would surprise the listeners, his method of payment would have been far more of a shock!

20:8 *When evening came.* This would be at dusk. The laborer's day went from sunrise to sunset.

beginning with the last ones hired and going on to the first. This arrangement sets up the scene that assures the confrontation of verses 11–12.

20:9–12 Probably those hired last agreed to the same arrangement with the landowner as those hired at the third hour (i.e., they would be paid "whatever is right"—v. 4). As they receive a denarius for an hour's work, they would have been joyfully surprised. Quite naturally, the spirits of the others in line would suddenly rise as they would assume their wages would be based on the same generous nature of the master—if those who worked only one hour or so received a denarius, what might those who had worked all day receive? Instead, as the foreman continues to pay each one a denarius, the earlier workers grow angry at the master. What at first seemed like a just and fair wage to which they could agree (v. 2) now appeared to them to be unjust and insulting.

20:12 *you have made them equal to us.* This is the crux of the complaint. The laborers assumed a hierarchal relationship to the master. Since they had been involved in working for him all day long, surely their reward ought to be greater than those who only got involved in the final hour. The parable shows that a concern for reward based on merit rather than on the grace of the master (God) is inappropriate in the kingdom.

20:13 *Friend.* In the other places where this form of address is used (Matt. 22:12; 26:50), it has an ironic twist to it. The laborers are not relating to the landowner as a friend, but as an unjust man.

I am not being unfair to you. The laborers' expressed concern was for justice. The landowner's point was that his actions were not unjust, since he was paying them what they had agreed to in the beginning. His generosity to the others cannot be interpreted as unfairness to them since he has fulfilled his promise to them.

20:15 *Don't I have the right to do what I want with my own money?* The landowner points out that he has the right to do what he will with his own money. The laborers are simply not in a position to tell him to whom he can or cannot be generous. In light of the ongoing conflict with the Pharisees regarding Jesus' interest in the religious outcasts of his time, Jesus, by means of this parable, "warns the Pharisees that a desire to live justly according to the covenant should not lead to an attitude that dictates to the covenant God how mercy and generosity should be shown. The line between following God's will and deciding what God wills is always thin and fragile" (Donahue).

20:16 This line, in reverse order of that in Matthew 19:30, connects the parable with the scene in 19:28–30. The promise that the disciples will judge over Israel (19:28) is not to be made into a new battleground for positions of status. The disciples are not to lord over one another (Matt. 20:25), but are to live as servants of God's people (Matt. 20:28).

UNIT 12—Parable of the Ten Virgins / Matt. 25:1–13

The Parable of the Ten Virgins

25 *"At that time the kingdom of heaven will be like ten virgins who took their lamps and went out to meet the bridegroom.* ²*Five of them were foolish and five were wise.* ³*The foolish ones took their lamps but did not take any oil with them.* ⁴*The wise, however, took oil in jars along with their lamps.* ⁵*The bridegroom was a long time in coming, and they all became drowsy and fell asleep.*

⁶*"At midnight the cry rang out: 'Here's the bridegroom! Come out to meet him!'*

⁷*"Then all the virgins woke up and trimmed their lamps.* ⁸*The foolish ones said to the wise, 'Give us some of your oil; our lamps are going out.'*

⁹*" 'No,' they replied, 'there may not be enough for both us and you. Instead, go to those who sell oil and buy some for yourselves.'*

¹⁰*"But while they were on their way to buy the oil, the bridegroom arrived. The virgins who were ready went in with him to the wedding banquet. And the door was shut.*

¹¹*"Later the others also came. 'Sir! Sir!' they said. 'Open the door for us!'*

¹²*"But he replied, 'I tell you the truth, I don't know you.'*

¹³*"Therefore keep watch, because you do not know the day or the hour."*

READ

First Reading / First Impressions: What made the "wise virgins" different than the "foolish virgins"?

❒ They had been Girl Scouts.

❒ They didn't fall asleep.

❒ They were always prepared.

❒ They made responsible decisions.

Second Reading / Big Idea: What are two key ideas you see here?

SEARCH

1. This is the first of three parables Matthew includes in his extended discourse on the final judgment (24:1–25:46). In this parable, there are two categories of people awaiting the bridegroom: wise virgins and foolish virgins. What behavior makes one type wise and the other foolish?

2. What point is Jesus (the Bridegroom) making about the timing of his return to earth (vv. 5a,6; see notes)?

3. Why didn't the five prepared virgins share their oil with the foolish virgins (vv. 7–9)? Were they being selfish (see note on v. 9)?

56

4. What happens to the five virgins who are unprepared for the delayed return of the bridegroom?

5. What warning is Jesus giving us in verse 13 about when he will come and what we need to do?

6. The wise virgins were prepared for the bridegroom's coming because they had a supply of oil. What "oil" must we have a supply of in our "lamps" in order to be properly prepared for Christ's coming (see note on v. 8)?

APPLY

1. What is your response to the fact that the five unprepared virgins were not allowed into the banquet? What do you think about the implication that there is a limit to God's open door of grace?
   ❑ Justice: What you sow is what you reap.
   ❑ Compassion: I wish they had had more sense.
   ❑ Anger: Everyone should be allowed in.
   ❑ Thankfulness: We should just be grateful that people get invited at all.
   ❑ Fairness: They had their chance.
   ❑ Detachment: I'm not sure—I'm glad it's God's business.
   ❑ Confusion: I'm unsure what "oil" we need to have to be ready.
   ❑ other:_____

2. This parable points out the seriousness of being ready for the final Day of the Lord. The "wise" have sought and received God's grace for redemption. The "foolish" have never sought God's grace for the forgiveness of sin. Which of the two types of people do you identify with most? (Circle one.)

Prepared for Christ's return　　　　　　　　　　　　　　　　　**Unprepared for Christ's return**

3. If you knew (even though no one "knows the day or the hour") that Jesus was returning in a very short period of time, how would you live your life differently?

GROUP AGENDA

After the first part, read the Scripture out loud and divide into groups of 4. Then come back together for the third part.

TO BEGIN / 10–15 Min. (Choose 1 or 2)

1. Have you ever been at a wedding where things went really wrong? How about your own?

2. What happened the last time your electricity went off? How prepared were you?

3. Are you usually early, late, or right on time? What about for this meeting?

TO GO DEEPER / 30 Min. (Choose 2 or 3)

1. What point stands out to you about this passage from the READ and SEARCH questions or the study notes?

2. Why do you think this parable was so important to Christians at the close of the first century—30 or 40 years after Jesus returned to heaven? Why should it be important today?

3. What does this parable add to the teaching about the Second Coming in 1 Thessalonians 4:13–18?

4. Have you in the past (or in the present) tried to live off the "oil" of someone else's faith? If so, whose—that of your parents? Spouse? Friends? Church? Small Group?

5. Quite frankly, does the fact that the Bible teaches that Jesus Christ will one day return affect the way you live your life today? If so, how?

6. CASE STUDY: Judy has always been cynical about the Christian teaching on heaven. But her teenage son was killed in a car accident recently, and she comes to you for comfort. What can you say to her?

TO CLOSE / 15–30 Min.

1. How are you doing on your group mission? Are you planning a kickoff for starting a new small group? Have you made plans for celebrating your time together as a group?

2. How did you answer the questions in APPLY, especially the second question?

3. How would you like the group to pray for you this week?

NOTES

Summary. This is the first of three parables in chapter 25 that deal with the return of the Lord on the Day of Judgment, a theme that dominates much of chapter 24 as well. The focus of this and the final two parables is on the need for the disciples to "keep watch" (v. 13), since the time for this day is unknown. The Parable of the Talents (25:14–30) stresses that watching means being occupied with investing one's God-given abilities in the work of the kingdom, while the final parable shows that such an investment means caring for the needy (25:31–46).

25:1 ten virgins. There is no attempt in the parable to impart any special meaning to the numbers 10 or five. They simply reflect two categories of people. It is not clear who these young women are: the attendants of the bride, servants in the groom's house, friends, or neighbors. In any case, their job is to escort the bridegroom in the wedding procession.

took their lamps. Since weddings typically occurred at night, lamps would both illuminate the bridal procession and add to the celebrative nature of the event. The lamps were probably small earthen jars with a wick inserted to draw the oil used as fuel. They would be held up on poles to brighten the way for the procession. Or they were torches made of rags wrapped around the end of a pole and soaked in oil. Such torches would burn for about 15 minutes and then would have to be dipped in oil again.

to meet the bridegroom. The parable is based upon common wedding practices of the time. Weddings typically took place in the house of the groom or in his parents' home. Prior to the actual ceremony, the groom would go to the home of the bride and lead her in a procession back to his house where the wedding would take place. In a village, the procession would be made up of everyone in the town! While commentators differ on the exact situation of these 10 women, a best guess is that they are either at the bride's house or are somewhere along the processional route waiting for the groom to come. In contrast to most other parables, the details of this parable are somewhat unrealistic (i.e., weddings did not occur at midnight; shops would not be open so late). This suggests that the parable is to be interpreted more as an allegory than is true for most of Jesus' parables. As an allegory, the parable likely follows the lead of the Old Testament in picturing God (or, in this context, the Messiah), as the groom coming to take Israel as his bride (Isa. 54:4–5; 62:4; Ezek. 16:7; Hos. 2:19).

25:2 foolish ... wise. In Old Testament usage, wise people are those who live in accordance with God's precepts. They make good choices in life because they put truth into practice. Fools are those who hear the truth but fail to act upon it (see also Matt. 7:24–27). The action of the foolish women in this parable is not an isolated event for them; rather it is indicative of the way they live their lives. They do not show forethought; they do not prepare for the future. In the context of the parable, they are like people who fail to be prepared for the coming of the Lord in judgment. Likewise, the wise women are habitually wise; in light of their future expectations, they make responsible decisions in the present.

25:3–4 did not take any oil. The only fuel for their lamps was whatever was left in the earthen lamps from the last use.

25:5 The bridegroom was a long time in coming. The early church expected Jesus to return in glory fairly soon after his ascension. Many of the parables related to his return can be seen as being intended to warn against that expectation (Matt. 24:43,48; 25:14ff). The time frame is ambiguous.

they all became drowsy and fell asleep. There is no suggestion that their falling asleep was inappropriate; it simply accents how long they had to wait.

25:6 At midnight. Just as it would be today, this was late for a wedding! It emphasizes how delayed the groom was in arriving, since this would have been long after most people would have expected him.

the cry rang out. In a village, everyone would be waiting for the celebration to begin. At first sight of the groom, the word would spread through the town.

Come out to meet him! People would gather around the groom to escort him to the bride's home and back to the site of the wedding. His unexpected arrival, the shout of proclamation, and the people coming out to meet him all suggest pictures used to describe Christ's return (see 1 Thess. 4:16–17).

25:7 trimmed their lamps. This is, literally, "put their torches in order." This would include dipping them in oil again or making sure there was oil in the lamps and then setting them alight for the procession. The lamps of the foolish virgins would not stay lit for lack of adequate oil.

25:8 our lamps are going out. Now that the time for the procession has arrived, the foolish women realize they do not have adequate supplies to keep their lamps burning. Following the allegorical interpretation of this parable, the lamps may be meant to indicate the good deeds of believers that spring from faith (see Matt. 5:16). The foolish women are those who have no good deeds with which to greet the Lord.

25:9 No. The wise women's refusal to share was not selfish, but simply prudent. They carried only enough for themselves. To share meant everyone would not have sufficient fuel. This aspect of the story is thought to show that each person needs his or her own relationship with the Lord; such a relationship cannot be obtained by simply being around those who demonstrate faith through faithful living.

go to those who sell oil. Since it is so late, it would be very difficult to find a shopkeeper willing to open shop and sell oil. At the time of the Lord's return, it is too late to try to make up for one's lack of preparation beforehand.

25:10 the wedding banquet. The image of a wedding feast was commonly used to describe God's salvation of his people (Mark 2:19; Luke 14:15).

the door was shut. Here the parable clearly moves from a story about a typical wedding to the messianic banquet, as latecomers would not be excluded from a regular wedding party. The shutting of the door to the banquet would strike the hearers as unusual, forcing them to consider the meaning of the parable. This aspect of the parable emphasizes the urgency of one's response to the Lord. There is a limited time when the "day of salvation" is extended to people: It must be received while the Lord provides the opportunity (see also Matt. 7:22–23; Luke 13:25).

25:12 When the foolish women finally arrived, they were forbidden entry.

I don't know you. See also Matthew 7:23 and Luke 13:25,27; the latter is found in a short parable that has similarities to the story of the 10 virgins. This is the final word of rejection from the Lord to those who fail to be ready for his coming. While they have the outward signs of commitment, their unpreparedness demonstrates their lack of taking his teachings seriously. In this context, not to be known does not mean that these women are not recognized, but that they are not really part of the company of people who are friends with the groom.

you do not know the day or the hour. This is a steady theme in the New Testament teachings about the return of the Lord (Matt. 24:36,44; Mark 13:35; Luke 12:40; 1 Thess. 5:1–2).

UNIT 13—Parable of the Weeds / Matt. 13:24-30,36-43

The Parable of the Weeds

²⁴Jesus told them another parable: "The kingdom of heaven is like a man who sowed good seed in his field. ²⁵But while everyone was sleeping, his enemy came and sowed weeds among the wheat, and went away. ²⁶When the wheat sprouted and formed heads, then the weeds also appeared.

²⁷"The owner's servants came to him and said, 'Sir, didn't you sow good seed in your field? Where then did the weeds come from?'

²⁸" 'An enemy did this,' he replied.

"The servants asked him, 'Do you want us to go and pull them up?'

²⁹" 'No,' he answered, 'because while you are pulling the weeds, you may root up the wheat with them. ³⁰Let both grow together until the harvest. At that time I will tell the harvesters: First collect the weeds and tie them in bundles to be burned; then gather the wheat and bring it into my barn.' " ...

The Parable of the Weeds Explained

³⁶Then he left the crowd and went into the house. His disciples came to him and said, "Explain to us the parable of the weeds in the field."

³⁷He answered, "The one who sowed the good seed is the Son of Man. ³⁸The field is the world, and the good seed stands for the sons of the kingdom. The weeds are the sons of the evil one, ³⁹and the enemy who sows them is the devil. The harvest is the end of the age, and the harvesters are angels.

⁴⁰"As the weeds are pulled up and burned in the fire, so it will be at the end of the age. ⁴¹The Son of Man will send out his angels, and they will weed out of his kingdom everything that causes sin and all who do evil. ⁴²They will throw them into the fiery furnace, where there will be weeping and gnashing of teeth. ⁴³Then the righteous will shine like the sun in the kingdom of the Father. He who has ears, let him hear."

READ

First Reading / First Impressions: What is the strongest impression you get having just read this parable?

- ❐ that Jesus has a devious enemy
- ❐ that a judgment time is coming
- ❐ that prior to the Judgment the world will remain a mixture of good and evil
- ❐ other:_____

Second Reading / Big Idea: Imagine you are a writer for the *National Enquirer*. Having heard Jesus teach, what sensational title for this parable would you come up with to grab the attention of people at the nation's checkout counters?

SEARCH

1. According to Jesus' interpretation (vv. 37–43), what do the various elements of the story represent?

- The sower of good seed is _____
- The sower of bad seed is _____
- The field is _____
- The harvest time is _____
- The good plants are _____
- The harvesters are_____
- The weeds are _____

2. What do you suppose would be the motivation of the enemy in sowing weeds into another person's field (see note on v. 25)? What do you suppose would be the motivation of the devil in sowing weeds into God's kingdom?

Human Enemy's Motive	The Devil's Motive

3. Why would the owner of the field not want his servants to pull out the weeds (see notes on v. 29 and v. 30)?

4. What does this imply about the way people of the kingdom should relate to the rest of the people in the world (see note on 13:24–30)?

5. What will happen to the "weeds" and the "wheat" when they are separated at the "harvest" (see notes on v. 42 and v. 43)?

APPLY

1. What do you think is the most important application of this parable for the church today?

2. What role do you think Jesus does NOT want you to play in his kingdom?

3. What role do you think Jesus DOES want you to play in a world that is filled with wheat and weeds?

GROUP AGENDA

After the first part, read the Scripture out loud and divide into groups of 4. Then come back together for the third part.

TO BEGIN / 10–15 Min. (Choose 1 or 2)
1. Among your family and friends, who is the best practical joker?

2. How are you at growing weeds? What weed grows best in your yard?

3. On a scale from 1 to 10, how much delight could you get from pulling weeds?

TO GO DEEPER / 30 Min. (Choose 2 or 3)
1. Based on the homework and study notes, what was the big point Jesus was making in this parable?

2. Why do Christians struggle with patience and tolerance toward others, specifically unbelievers? Why do you?

3. In what way can overzealous judgment of the world and individuals harm our mission as believers?

4. On the other hand, how do you balance the teaching of this parable with Matthew 18:17 and 1 Corinthians 5:1–2?

5. According to polls, the majority of Americans claim they have a religious faith and attend church at least occasionally. Yet the church seems to have little influence on society. How do you account for this?

6. CASE STUDY: Some of the baby boomers who have started coming to your church have brought their "New Age" teachings with them. They want to be members of your church, but they do not believe in the essentials of the faith (like the Apostles' Creed). What do you do?

TO CLOSE / 15–30 Min.
1. From the APPLY section of the homework, what is the message in this parable for the church? For you?

2. What have you gained the most from this study of Parables? What was the "serendipity" of this course—the unexpected blessing?

3. Have you finalized your plans for the future of your group?

4. How can this group remember you in prayer?

NOTES

Summary. The Parable of the Weeds is the first of three parables about the growth of the kingdom. It is followed by the Parable of the Mustard Seed (Matt. 13:31–32) and the Parable of the Yeast (Matt. 13:33). All communicate that the kingdom of God will assuredly grow, although by a process that is hard to discern (and may at first look ineffectual).

13:24–30 The issue to which this parable speaks is the fact that (contrary to popular opinion), the kingdom of God will not be ushered in suddenly, with a great cataclysmic explosion. Popular expectation held that God's kingdom would be established by means of a dramatic act of judgment that would divide humanity into two camps: the sons of light and the sons of darkness. With the coming of Jesus, however, life appeared to go on much as it always had. There was no apocalyptic revelation of God, no war that wiped out the wicked, no sudden deliverance for the righteous. Some people believed and practiced what he taught and others did not ... and nothing happened to those who didn't! Even more confusing, within his ranks there were some whose allegiance was questionable. How could Jesus claim to be the herald of God's kingdom? Yet in him the kingdom is begun. However, its full nature and extent will not be made known until the Day of Judgment. For the time being, the kingdom of God is hidden and his disciples must not be occupied with thoughts of how to purify it by their own efforts. God will take that action at the time of the final judgment. An explanation for the parable is given in verses 36–43.

13:24 *Jesus told them another parable.* In Matthew, this parable follows the Parable of the Sower. Both parables use an agricultural image to teach about the certain growth and productivity of the kingdom of God.

The kingdom of heaven. In their desire not to take the name of the Lord their God in vain (Ex. 20:7), Jews avoided direct references to God at all. Instead, they would refer to God through a phrase like "the One in heaven." The "kingdom of heaven" is simply a substitution for the "kingdom of God."

13:25 *sleeping.* This does not suggest inattention, but simply normal rest. It is the same as saying that the deed was done "at night."

weeds. This was probably darnel, a poisonous weed that looks like wheat until the time when the head forms on the wheat. Sowing a field with useless seed was a common means by which a disgruntled person might seek revenge upon an enemy, since such a sowing could devastate a crop. To sow darnel among wheat was forbidden by Roman law.

13:27 *didn't you sow good seed.* "The question, although quite natural from the agricultural point of view, may also indicate the application of the parable to the situation of the church of Matthew's day. It was probably experiencing concern at the apparent lack of triumph and progress in the world of the kingdom inaugurated by Jesus" (Hill).

13:29 It might have been possible to pull out the darnel when it was young. However, its close resemblance to wheat meant that some of the young wheat would inadvertently get uprooted as well. When the plant was more mature—especially if there were a lot of it—its root system would be so intertwined with that of the wheat that to uproot it would also uproot a good bit of the wheat. Thus, the owner of the field chooses to do nothing. He neither tries to pull out the weeds, nor seeks to find out who did this so that he might get revenge. To the surprise of his servants (and the hearers of the story), he simply allows the wheat and the weeds to grow up together.

13:30 Only at the time of the harvest, when the fruit of each plant was clearly visible, would the weeds be separated from the wheat. The darnel (sometimes used for fuel when there was a shortage of wood) would be burned up while the wheat would go into the barn for storage and later use.

13:36–43 One of Matthew's themes is the coming judgment of God, in which the righteous will be vindicated and the wicked punished (3:7–12; 7:24–27; 10:23; 11:20–24; 18:7–9; 22:1–14; 24:1–51; 25:31–46). This was an important expectation for the Jewish communities of the time and was embraced by many of the early Christians as well. Such a destiny calls for repentance and a life of obedience to God.

13:37–39 What the various elements of the parable mean are explained.

13:37 *the Son of Man.* This is an allusion to the heavenly figure in Daniel 7:13–14, who is given authority by God over all of the world.

13:38 *the world.* This is secular reality; it refers to the present age.

sons of the kingdom. These are the people who have been given the gift of the kingdom (Matt. 5:3). To be a "son" of something or someone meant to be a person who reflects the characteristics of that particular thing or person. The "sons of the kingdom" are people whose lives are in conformity to the values of that kingdom. The "sons of the evil one" are those whose character reflects that of Satan.

13:39 *The harvest.* Picturing God's final judgment in terms of a harvest was a common metaphor in the Old Testament and other apocalyptic literature (Isa. 17:4–6; Jer. 51:33; Joel 3:12–13).

the end of the age. Apocalyptic literature viewed history in terms of "the present age" and "the age to come." The present age is marked by sin and the oppression of the righteous, but the "age to come" will begin when God dramatically puts an end to this age by his judgment and eradication of evil, ushering in a new age in which he reigns over all with justice and peace.

angels. Angels figure prominently in apocalyptic scenes of God's judgment as the agents through which that judgment is executed (v. 41; Dan. 7:10; 2 Thess. 1:7; Rev. 15:1; 16:1; 18:1,21).

13:40 *burned in the fire.* God's judgment was often described in terms of a consuming fire that would purify the world of all evil (2 Thess. 1:7; 2 Peter 3:10; Rev. 19:20).

13:41 The Son of Man, who sowed the good seed (v. 37), is also the one who harvests the crop and owns the kingdom.

13:42 *weeping and gnashing of teeth.* This is a stock phrase used to indicate the extreme horror and suffering of those who experience God's wrath. In Matthew, such a punishment is described in terms of a fire (here and 13:50), darkness (8:12; 22:13; 25:30), and being cut to pieces (24:51).

13:43 *the righteous.* These are the "sons of the kingdom" (v. 38) who heard the word and practiced it. Although their identity was once hidden (when the wheat and the weeds were growing together), they will be fully revealed in the age to come as those who share God's character.

shine like the sun. Light is often used to describe the nature of holiness. It is a positive characteristic, as opposed to the darkness that marks the nature of sin (Dan. 12:3; 1 John 1:5).

He who has ears, let him hear. This is another stock phrase used to call people to think about what they have heard: What does it mean? What are its implications? How are we to act upon this story? The worst condition to be in is one in which we hear Jesus' words but fail to let them have an effect on our lives.

COMMENTS
"Let both grow together until the harvest."

"... The visible church is to have its intermixture of good and bad until the end of time, and by consequence ... the fact of the bad being found mingled with the good will in no wise justify a separation from it, or an attempt to set up a little Church of our own. Where men attempt this ... it is not difficult to see what fatal effects on their own spiritual life it must have, what darkness it must bring upon them, and into what a snare of pride it must cast them. For while even in the best men there is the same intermixture of good and evil as there is outwardly in the Church, such conduct will infallibly lead a man to the willful shutting his eyes both to the evil which is in himself, and in the little schismatical body he will then call the Church, since only so the attempt will even seem to be successful.

"Not that there is not something in every man which inclines him to (this) error ... Nay, it would argue little love or holy earnestness in him, if he had not this longing to see the Church of his Savior a glorious Church without spot or wrinkle. But he must learn that the desire, righteous and holy as in itself it is, yet is not to find its fulfillment in this present evil time ... He learns that all self-willed and impatient attempts, such as have been repeated again and again, to anticipate that perfect communion of saints are indeed works of the flesh, and that however well they may promise at the first, no blessing will rest upon them, nor will they for long even appear to be attended with success" (Richard Trench, *Notes on the Parables of Our Lord*, New York: D. Appleton and Co., 1864, pp. 85–86).